Improve Your Eyesight with EFT*

*Emotional Freedom Techniques

Carol Look, EFT Master

Bloomington, IN  Milton Keynes, UK

authorHOUSE®

AuthorHouse™
1663 Liberty Drive, Suite 200
Bloomington, IN 47403
www.authorhouse.com
Phone: 1-800-839-8640

AuthorHouse™ UK Ltd.
500 Avebury Boulevard
Central Milton Keynes, MK9 2BE
www.authorhouse.co.uk
Phone: 08001974150

First published by AuthorHouse 7/17/2006

ISBN: 1-4259-4958-4 (sc)

Printed in the United States of America
Bloomington, Indiana

This book is printed on acid-free paper.

DISCLAIMER

EFT (Emotional Freedom Techniques) is a member of a new class of treatment techniques and protocols referred to as **Energy Therapy.** While still considered *experimental*, these techniques are being used by therapists, nurses, physicians, psychiatrists and lay people worldwide. To date, **EFT** and other **Energy Therapy Techniques** have yielded exceptional results in the treatment of psychological and physical problems. They are *NOT* meant to replace appropriate medical treatment or mental health therapy. Personally, I have not experienced any adverse side effects when applying these techniques and when the treatment protocols and suggestions were followed. This does not mean, however, that you or your clients will not experience or perceive negative side effects. *If you use these techniques on yourself or others, you must agree to take full responsibility for your own well-being and you are required to advise your clients to do the same. You may NOT hold EFT Founder, Gary Craig, or the author, Carol Look, responsible/ liable for any side effects you experience as a result of using these techniques.*

Table of Contents

FOREWORD

by Dr. Patricia Carrington

As a clinical psychologist and researcher long aware of mind-body interactions, I have been watching with special interest the effects of applying the simple acupuncture-related technique, **Emotional Freedom Techniques (EFT)**, to eyesight problems, and feel compelled to ask you these questions as I introduce this exceptional book.

Question 1: Do you see your eyesight as influenced by your response to your environment, either physical or emotional, or do you see it as a more or less unchangeable physical condition (i.e. as either black or white ––you either have good vision or you don't; you either need some sort of lenses or you don't)?

Question 2: What do you expect from your vision as you get older?

Question 3: How do you see nature's healing processes as applied to the state of your vision, now or in the future? Are you only hoping to neutralize your eyesight problems in one way or another but never really cure them?

In a book written many years ago, the then Director of the General Electric Company's Lighting Research Laboratory, Dr. Matthew Luckiesh, asked his readers to imagine what would happen if "crippled" eyes "could be transformed into crippled legs." His comments were: "If this (transformation) happened, what a heartrending parade we would witness on a busy street! Nearly every other person would go limping by. Many would be on crutches and some in wheelchairs." He was at that time referring to the widespread use of eyeglasses (now we would add to this the even more widespread use of contact lenses) on a

PERMANENT basis, as usually being the sole treatment for eyesight problems. Many years later, that is still, regrettably, the case.

If it is legs that are crippled, however, doctors typically refuse to let their patients rely just on crutches. They regard the use of crutches as a necessary temporary strategy, and while paying attention to external conditions, they do their best to improve the *internal* conditions of the defective limbs, so that nature is allowed to do its work of healing.

If respect for the power of natural healing is applied to our limbs, why is a similar respect for the recuperative powers of the human body not applied to defective eyesight? This question is not generally asked by the medical establishment which, until now, has simply taken it for granted that defective eyesight is incurable and inevitable with age, and this is in spite of the eye's demonstrably close relationship with the mind and the emotions. It is not generally assumed that eyesight can return to normalcy through improvement within the mind-body sphere, and you yourself may unwittingly have adopted this point of view, as do most people.

This book therefore presents a radically new approach to defective vision and for this reason requires somewhat of a leap of faith. To change one's eyesight by behavioral means (i.e. **EFT** in this case) seems impossible in terms of what we have been told countless times. Yet the fact is that psychological experiments have determined that the act of seeing involves consciousness and that in fact our perceptions and our emotions are intrinsically linked.

Consider for example the statement, "He/she made me so mad I couldn't see straight!" This refers to the effects of anger on the focusing and flexibility of the eyes. In fact, studies have shown that anger can actually redden the eyes and swell the minor blood vessels. Rage can also cause the vision to blur and "warp" so that the person actually "can't see straight" when they are too angry.

When you are working with the exercises in this book you will notice an exercise involving the expression of anger and you may be startled when you discover the usefulness of **EFT** for that emotion and the beneficial impact of this anger exercise on your eyesight.

Because seeing and human consciousness are so intimately linked, it is not surprising that sadness, fear, discouragement and other negative emotions affect your eyes almost instantly. Tension is intensified in the eyes within a split-second if you experience any form of emotional distress and it is manifested as tight lids and tight muscles. Tense facial muscles often create a furrow between the eyebrows in an effort to relieve inner discomfort adding a further difficulty, and tense eye muscles then create congestion, which leads to restricted circulation in the region of the eyes and greatly lessened oxygen supply to the eyes, etc.

On the other side of the equation however, you may have noticed how your eyes shine when you are happy or inspired. The eyes of a little child sparkle when an unexpected treat or gift is given, and this kind of sparkle should be the natural healthy state of your eyes.

The fact is that, whether caused by hidden inner tensions or an outer challenge, tension in the eyes dulls the vision and can be the beginning of organic as well as functional problems. Here we have the relationship between our eyesight and the emotions and the reason why a method such as **EFT**, which has a capacity to deeply influence our emotions and change our entire adjustment to life, can be of immense help in reversing tension-caused defects in eyesight. By using **EFT** to target emotions that may cause you to withdraw from contact with others or with life around you, **EFT** can actually reverse the tendency of your eyes to withdraw from contact with the world around you ——a primary cause of defective vision that has been addressed in the mind-body field but generally neglected by mainstream medicine.

In this right-on-target book Dr. Carol Look takes you by the hand and guides you through what we might ironically call an "eye opening experience," as you confront some of the inner blocks that have prevented you from experiencing full vision of your world.

This, of course, requires you to be open to what will happen when the exercises start working. My advice is to take as non-judgmental an attitude as possible toward the exercises you will be doing, adopting an open-minded "let's see" approach. If you are able to go with the flow from exercise to exercise, and explore the use of **EFT** for the emotions and attitudes that are most likely to be causing your faulty vision, you may be startled by the improvement that occurs in your eyesight. You will no longer need the "protection" of a dimmed-out view of the world.

While this may seem to require a certain amount of blind faith, in actual fact it only requires you to do the exercises and see what happens. In short, this book is an experiment from beginning to end. One of the most interesting results of the experiment conducted by Carol Look was the degree to which deeper issues in the lives of those who participated in it were automatically addressed and this improved both their lives AND their vision at the same time. As each emotional issue became resolved, the eyesight tended to improve. This is a fascinating outcome.

However, like all beneficial health programs, you must DO IT in order to get the results you want. You must stick with the exercises, even on days when they may be a bit (or sometimes quite) emotionally uncomfortable. You must not let comfort be your criteria but instead allow healing to prevail. This book's exercises should be a true adventure for you. Not knowing just what will be around the next corner, I suggest you just plunge in and work those emotional muscles of yours. The payoff will be tremendous. You will be exploring a greatly expanded personal vision on all levels.

Patricia Carrington Ph.D.

Associate Clinical Professor

UMDNJ-Robert Wood Johnson Medical School

Piscataway, NJ

*(Dr. Carrington is one of the small group of **EFT** Practitioners worldwide to qualify as **EFT Masters**. She is the originator of the widely acclaimed **EFT Choices Method** (www.eftupdate.com)*

INTRODUCTION

When **EFT** Founder Gary Craig raised the topic of vision improvement using **EFT**, I was momentarily skeptical, and then I remembered how many of my clients have remarked after rounds of **EFT**, *"Everything looks brighter to me now..."* or *"Now I see more clearly."* The idea began to make more and more sense....why wouldn't our fear, guilt, anger and shame show up in our vision? These emotions apparently show up in every other part of our anatomy and physiology, why not in our eyesight?

I was very eager to launch the free experiment in the Fall of 2005 to see what the results would be. Considering that few doctors or lay people even entertain the idea that our eyesight could be improved by balancing our energy system, the final results of the experiment were nothing short of fantastic. (The entire "experiment paper" is included in this book at the end of the assignments.)

Approximately 75% of those participants that completed the before and after questionnaire reported somewhere between a 15-75% improvement in their vision....just from tapping on acupressure points while focusing on their emotions!

I am very grateful to the more than 100 people who tenaciously stuck with the experiment and tapped every day on guilt, anger, shame or other conflicts that were "hidden" in their eyesight. Even after dozens of people begged me to let them "join" the experiment after the cutoff date was announced, three-quarters of the original group dropped out. I received numerous emails saying "life got in the way." Others admitted that they were not patient enough to follow through, while still others were frightened by the changes they were experiencing. Several participants wrote me saying they didn't want to pay for new prescriptions (which, by the way, seemed inevitable) so they stopped doing their daily routines.

Bear in mind that the **EFT setup phrases** I devised for the 8 weeks of experiment assignments were often rather emotionally charged or "heavy" and I was unable to give individualized attention to these participants. Overall, I am basically not surprised by the non-compliance; this is not highly unusual for people who embark on self-help journeys on their own when results are neither immediate nor dramatic in the beginning. Again, I was unable to help them if any secondary gains or conflicts --- what I call the possible *downside to seeing more clearly* --- surfaced.

Before the experiment was even completed, friends and colleagues encouraged me by saying, "you have to make this into a book!" So here it is, the original **EFT Eyesight Experiment**, so that you may do the exercises at your own pace. You may complete the progress charts in your own time as well.

The series of emails I sent to participants over the 8 week period are for the most part, intact. Other than deleting excessively repetitious directions and web links that are no longer working, you will be reading what the actual participants read each Monday morning for 2 months, with a few "reminder" emails thrown in. (After you have completed the official assignments, I highly recommend that you to continue using **EFT** for any emotions or conflicts that may inhibit your vision or interfere with your basic well-being.)

Please go at your own pace! This is not a race or a contest, this is an *invitation* to improve your vision by releasing the pent up emotions stored in your eyes.

Enjoy,

Carol Look

ACKNOWLEDGEMENTS

A special thanks to **EFT** founder Gary Craig, who had the vision and passion to create **EFT**, and the generosity to make it widely available to all of us. (http://www.emofree.com)

Many thanks to my friend and colleague Jayne Morgan-Kidd who *donated* hours and hours of her time analyzing the incoming data and compiling the statistics for the final report. (http://www. jaynemorgankidd.com)

I am deeply grateful to my friend and trusted colleague Rick Wilkes who, as usual, gave me exceptional guidance and supported me through this entire process. (http://www.ThrivingNow.com)

I am so appreciative of Dr. Patricia Carrington's compassion, wisdom, and dependability. She provided excellent editorial and emotional support. (http://www.EFTupdate.com)

Many thanks to my patient and loving family members who understand my passion for **EFT** and tolerated the endless hours I spent setting up, administering, and completing this project.

EFT

EYESIGHT

EXPERIMENT

INSTRUCTIONS

INSTRUCTIONS

Hi everyone,

Welcome to the **EFT EYESIGHT EXPERIMENT.**

If you decide to use the EFT suggestions in this experiment, you are hereby agreeing to take full responsibility for yourself and your emotional and physical well-being.

In order for the collected data to be as accurate as possible, you need to follow some basic directions. They are as follows:

(1) **Get your eyes tested before and after the 8 week experiment,** *or* **devise your own "test" that can be accurately repeated before and after each week and/or before and after the experiment.** (For example, measure the distance between where you are standing and printed words on a poster on the wall, record how well you can see it, test before and after...)

(2) **Keep good records of how many times a week you complete the 5 minutes of recommended EFT exercises. I need to know if you completed the exercises only once a week, 3 times or 5 times a week. I hope you will complete them 7 times a week, but I need to know exact statistics. Don't let embarrassment about "forgetting" or "resisting" get in the way of completing the forms. I need it all.**

(3) **If you need extra emotional support, please work with a competent EFT practitioner. Remember, we will be addressing some** *charged* **emotional issues. This is a huge undertaking for me, and I am donating my time.**

I will not be providing extra support. See http://www.emofree.com for recommended practitioners.

(4)   Do not start taking any new supplements, eye drops, medications, or other treatments, alternative or traditional, that are supposed to help your eyes *unless recommended by your doctor.* Otherwise, this will skew the results of the experiment.

(5)   Do the EFT exercises in a quiet, private place, once a day for at least 5 minutes.

(6)   Record at least 2 of your impressions and improvements each week and write in the "comments" section on the questionnaire. (For example, Monday, week #1: *"I could see writing on page of book from 3 inches further away"*… or *"I was able to see colors clearer after EFT exercises."*)

(7)   Complete the questionnaire for yourself each week. I will be providing a link for you where you may input your data at the end of the 8 week experiment.

I will be sending you EFT setup phrases each week on Mondays.

When new aspects surface, which they will, please use the basics of EFT to pursue the line of thinking or feeling that came up for you. (Please refer to Gary Craig's basic manual or his beginning CDs and DVDs.)

I will *not* be reminding you to do your EFT exercises. If you find you have "forgotten" them more than once, this is good evidence that you have some resistance to getting over this problem.

Many thanks for agreeing to participate. I can't wait to *see* what the findings show us!

EFT

EYESIGHT

EXPERIMENT

QUESTIONNAIRE

QUESTIONNAIRE

PRINT OUT and FILL IN ALL INFORMATION BELOW.

KEEP FOR YOUR RECORDS.

You will be asked to input data AT THE END OF THE 8 week period.

FEMALE _____ MALE _____AGE_____

I had my eyes examined within the last 3 months _____yes _____no

My current prescription is _____

I wear glasses_____yes _____no/ contact lenses _____yes _____no

I have had lasik surgery_____yes _____no

I have had other eye surgery (please specify)

Please report any relevant diagnosis from your doctor: (glaucoma, macular degeneration, corneal issues, etc.)

Fill out the form below after each week of EFT exercises. At the end of the 8 weeks, you will be asked to complete a data entry form on the website.

- Please indicate how many times a week you completed the suggested EFT exercises (from 1-7 days)

- Please rate each row on the left (clarity, color, depth, fatigue) for each of the 8 weeks from a "0" to "5" as follows:

0 = no change
1 = very little change/improvement (up to 15%)
2 = slight improvement (15-25%)
3 = noticeable improvement (25-50%)
4 = definite improvement (50-75%)
5 = significant improvement (75% or more)

YOUR START DATE _____/END DATE_____

	Week 1	Week 2	Week 3	Week 4	Week 5	Week 6	Week 7	Week 8
# times per week I used the EFT exercises								
Brightness								
Color Contrast								
Color Perception								
Dryness								
Clarity (near)								
Clarity (far)								
Eye Fatigue								
Eye Burning/ itching								
Eye Strain								
Floaters?								

THE

BASICS

OF

EFT

Emotional

Freedom

Techniques (EFT)

BASICS OF
EMOTIONAL FREEDOM TECHNIQUES
(EFT)

For those of you who are new to **EFT**, I have included some simple directions which are variations of **EFT** founder Gary Craig's original "Basic Recipe."

You will also find a chart of the **EFT** acupressure points for tapping.

For thorough instruction in **EFT**, please consult Gary Craig's basic manual, a free download, at http://www.emofree.com.

DIRECTIONS:

A modified version of the basic **EFT** "recipe" consists of the following ingredients:

> **(1) THE SETUP STATEMENT**: (naming the problem combined with a general affirmation phrase)

> **(2) NEGATIVE TAPPING SEQUENCE (Round #1):** This consists of tapping the sequence of **8 EFT** points while you *focus on the problem* and say the *Reminder Phrase* out loud. (This helps you *tune in* to the problem.)

> **(3) POSITIVE TAPPING SEQUENCE (Round #2):** Tap on the sequence of the **8 EFT** "power points" again, and *focus on a solution* by verbalizing preferences, choices, and possible alternative outcomes.

THE SETUP STATEMENT:

THE SETUP <u>Statement</u> sounds like this:

*"Even though I have **this anxiety about tomorrow's meeting,** I deeply and completely love and accept myself."*

The **SETUP STATEMENT** is repeated out loud while you tap the **karate chop point (KC)** (see diagram of points).

<u>THE REMINDER PHRASE</u> sounds like this:

"This anxiety about tomorrow's meeting."

The REMINDER PHRASE is repeated when you tap the sequence of points. It helps you stay focused on the issue you have chosen for treatment.

NEGATIVE TAPPING SEQUENCE:

- **Starting at the eyebrow point,** begin tapping each point in the sequence of **EFT** points (see below) approximately 7 to 10 times while repeating the *negative reminder phrase*.

SEQUENCE OF TAPPING POINTS: (see diagram)

▪ Eyebrow (EB)	▪ Chin (CH)
▪ Side of Eye (SE)	▪ Collarbone (CB)
▪ Under Eye (UE)	▪ Under Arm (UA)
▪ Under Nose (UN)	▪ Top of Head (H)

- This directs your mind to focus on the negative thought patterns that block your ability to reach your goals (or feel calm, attract abundance, release food cravings) and **allows EFT to neutralize them.**

POSITIVE TAPPING SEQUENCE:

- **Starting at the eyebrow point again,** tap each of the 8 **EFT** points approximately 7-10 times while *repeating any sequence of positive phrases* you choose.

- **This allows you to install what you would *prefer* to experience emotionally in your thought patterns and in your life.**

DEEP BREATH:

- **Complete each exercise with a slow deep breath to help move the energy through your body.**

EFT DIRECTIONS

(1)   **CHOOSE AN ISSUE TO TREAT WITH EFT**

(2)   **Scale the intensity of the issue you have chosen to treat on a scale of 0-10** (where 0=no discomfort and 10=strong discomfort).

(3)   **Devise a SETUP STATEMENT for the issue you have chosen.** For instance, suppose you have chosen your fear about seeing your life more clearly. Your **SETUP STATEMENT** would sound like this: *"Even though I'm afraid to see my life more clearly, I deeply and completely love and accept myself anyway."*

(4)   **Tap on the Karate Chop Point while saying the SETUP STATEMENT out loud 3 times.**

(5)   **NEGATIVE TAPPING SEQUENCE: (ROUND #1): Tap on the sequence of points (see page 17) while repeating the NEGATIVE REMINDER PHRASE out loud. (*I'm afraid to see my life more clearly.*)**

(6)   **POSITIVE TAPPING SEQUENCE (ROUND #2): Tap on the sequence of points again while saying positive statements about what you want instead, what you choose, or what you intend.**

(7)   **Take a deep breath.**

(8)   **Check the rating of the intensity of the original emotion you had about this issue on the scale from 0-10 to see if it has changed.**

(9)   **Repeat steps 1-8 if necessary.**

EFT TAPPING POINTS

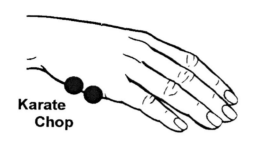

Karate Chop

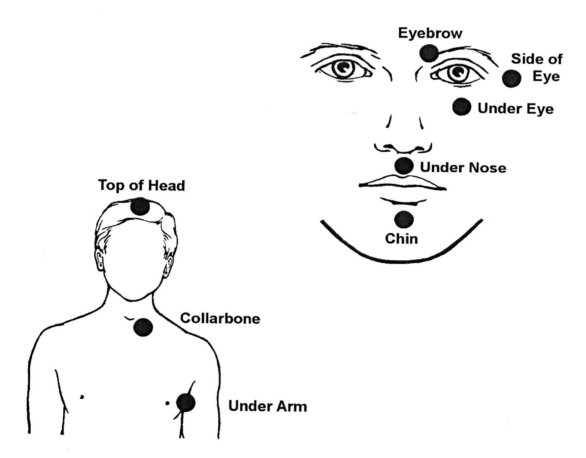

Eyebrow

Side of Eye

Under Eye

Under Nose

Top of Head

Chin

Collarbone

Under Arm

THE

EFT

EYESIGHT

EXPERIMENT

BEFORE YOU BEGIN WEEK #1

By now, you have all read the **directions** for the **EFT Eyesight Experiment**.

BEFORE YOU BEGIN:

Have you established a *baseline* for your vision? This can be done in 3 ways: (1) have your eyes checked and get your doctor's prescription, (2) devise a self-made test that can be measured before and after the tapping suggestions, or (3) use the eye test that can be self-administered from your computer screen which can be found at this following link: http://transportation.ky.gov/drlic/eye_test.htm.

Have you printed out your questionnaire?

Please scale the following emotional states on day #1 of the 8 week experiment, and again, after the 8 weeks are over on a scale of 0-10; "0" if you never feel this way, and "10" if you are quick to feel the emotion *all the time*.

(1) I feel angry
(2) I feel guilty easily
(3) I feel so hurt
(4) I feel resentful about so many things
(5) I feel ashamed of myself
(6) I have all these aches and pains

(I will incorporate any findings from this additional data into the final results.)

In the next section you will find TAPPING RECOMMENDATIONS for Week #1.

Print out this week's suggestions and use them in a private, quiet place for **at least 5 minutes a day**. Of course you may tweak the language to suit your exact situation, but this wording is an important foundation for the rest of the experiment.

You are supposed to do the exercises WITHOUT any corrective lenses on. *This brings up the concern about how your eyes might naturally re-adjust back to your original prescription.* Please do not worry about this. What I suspect might happen is that somewhere during the experiment, you will notice that your eyes will *not* adjust so easily, *clear evidence of improvement*. Take note of this and you will be able to make comments about it as the experiment progresses.

Please keep exact records and fill in the questionnaire with the number of days per week you completed the assignments, and whether any eyesight measurements listed on the **questionnaire** change or not from week to week. (You may also indicate if measurements got worse or not.)

Register the improvements cumulatively, so that by the end of week #8, the number in the final box will represent your *total improvement* throughout the experiment.

(For instance, if your *perception of color* seemed approximately 10% clearer after week #1, you would assign it a value of "1" in the box provided. If during week #2, you have noticed even more improvement, and you are now at a 20% improvement overall, you would assign that box a value of "2" for the second week. If during week #3, you don't notice any more improvement, you will assign that box a value of "2" again, representing the cumulative 20% improvement.)

Thanks, and enjoy it.

Carol Look

WEEK #1

RESISTANCE
&
LIMITING BELIEFS

EFT
EYESIGHT
EXPERIMENT

WEEK #1:
RESISTANCE and LIMITING BELIEFS

If we don't deal with our resistance, there is no point to conducting this experiment! Ask yourself the following questions:

    (1)   What is the "downside" to improving my vision?
    (2)   What might change in my life that will be uncomfortable for me?
    (3)   How might my eyesight improvement "rock the boat" in my family or at work?
    (4)   Who might feel uncomfortable with my seeing more clearly?

Incorporate the answers to your questions into the tapping phrases below.

EFT ROUND #1

While tapping on the karate chop point, repeat the following phrases:

Even though I am resistant to improving my eyesight, I deeply and completely love and accept myself...Even though I don't really want to improve my vision, I choose to accept myself anyway...Even though I'm afraid to see more clearly, I accept and love all of me.

Then tap on the following points while saying the phrases listed below:

EYEBROW: *I have this resistance to improving my eyesight*

SIDE OF EYE: *I don't want to improve my eyesight*

UNDER EYE: *I am afraid to see more clearly*

UNDER NOSE: *I thought I wanted to see better*

CHIN: *I don't really want to see better*

COLLARBONE: *This resistance to clearing up my vision*

UNDER ARM: *I have this resistance to improving my eyesight*

HEAD: *I can't help this resistance*

Then start tapping again on the eyebrow point and repeat these positive phrases:

EYEBROW: *I will consider releasing the resistance*

SIDE OF EYE: *I can allow myself to get over this resistance*

UNDER EYE: *I choose to feel ready to release the resistance*

UNDER NOSE: *I feel free to release the resistance*

CHIN: *I choose to let go of this resistance*

COLLARBONE: *It feels so good to allow clarity into my life*

UNDER ARM: *I appreciate my eyesight and my eyes*

HEAD: *I am grateful for the clarity in my life*

EFT ROUND #2

While tapping on the karate chop point, repeat the following phrases:

Even though I am skeptical that this will work, I choose to do the exercises anyway...Even though my skepticism is really fear, I accept and love myself anyway...Even though I have doubts about EFT improving my eyesight, I choose to accept the possibility now.

Then tap on the following points while saying the phrases listed below:

EYEBROW: *I have this skepticism about EFT and my eyesight*

SIDE OF EYE: *I don't want to improve my eyesight*

UNDER EYE: *I am afraid to see more clearly*

UNDER NOSE: *This skepticism*

CHIN: *These doubts about this working*

COLLARBONE: *This resistance to clearing up my vision*

UNDER ARM: *I have this resistance to improving my eyesight*

HEAD: *I have so many doubts about this*

Then start tapping again on the eyebrow point and repeat these positive phrases:

EYEBROW: *I will consider being open to new possibilities*

SIDE OF EYE: *I can allow myself to release the resistance*

UNDER EYE: *I choose to release the doubts*

UNDER NOSE: *I feel freer already*

CHIN: *I choose to let go of this resistance*

COLLARBONE: *It feels so good to allow clarity into my life*

UNDER ARM: *I appreciate my eyesight and my eyes*

HEAD: *I am grateful for the clarity in my life*

EFT ROUND #3

While tapping on the karate chop point, repeat the following phrases:

Even though I don't believe eye problems can be reversed, so I doubt I can release mine, I deeply and completely love and accept myself anyway...Even though I don't believe this will work, I choose to accept and love myself anyway...Even though the truth is I'm afraid to see more clearly, I accept and love all of me no matter what.

Then tap on the following points while saying the phrases listed below:

EYEBROW: *I don't really believe I can improve my eyesight*

SIDE OF EYE: *I don't want to believe I can improve my eyesight*

UNDER EYE: *I am afraid to believe I can improve my vision*

UNDER NOSE: *I have so many limiting beliefs about eyesight*

CHIN: *I don't really want to see more clearly*

COLLARBONE: *I have so much resistance to clearing up my vision*

UNDER ARM: *This resistance to improving my eyesight*

HEAD: *I am surprised about this resistance and my limiting beliefs*

Then start tapping again on the eyebrow point and repeat these positive phrases:

EYEBROW: *I will consider releasing the resistance*

SIDE OF EYE: *I can allow myself to release this resistance*

UNDER EYE: *I choose to feel open to change*

UNDER NOSE: *I allow myself to release the limiting beliefs*

CHIN: *I choose to let go of this resistance*

COLLARBONE: *It feels right to be open to seeing more clearly*

UNDER ARM: *I appreciate my eyesight and my eyes*

HEAD: *I am grateful for the clarity in my life*

EFT
EYESIGHT
EXPERIMENT

REMINDER

Use the **EFT recommendations** every day for at least 5 minutes. Late starters may find the first week's **EFT recommendations** by accessing the beginning of this section.

For those of you who can't see/read the written phrases without your corrective lenses, *go ahead and wear them while you tap!!*

But your eye "test" must be performed without them, before and after.

For those of you who are not familiar with **EFT**, please go to **www. emofree.com** for the free downloadable manual or the excellent tutorial program. As I made clear in my original instructions, **I will not be answering any personal emails about the experiment or any questions about the basic EFT process.**

Thank you,
Carol Look
www.CarolLook.com

WEEK #2

FEAR

EFT

EYESIGHT

EXPERIMENT

WEEK #2

Remember to fill out your questionnaire before beginning the next 7 days.

YOU MUST COMPLETE 7 DAYS OF TAPPING BEFORE FILLING OUT THE QUESTIONNAIRE AND MOVING ON TO WEEK #2.

Thanks, and enjoy it.

Carol Look

EFT
EYESIGHT
EXPERIMENT

WEEK #2:

FEAR OF WHAT I SAW IN THE PAST

Choose 1 or 2 incidents from your past involving something *you saw*...use it as a jumping off point for the following EFT suggestions. Rate the feelings of discomfort about each incident on a scale of 0-10. Keep rating it and noticing any improvements. (If this is the time to consult an excellent EFT practitioner for extra support, please do so at www.emofree.com.

EFT ROUND #1

While tapping on the karate chop point, repeat the following phrases:

Even though I was so afraid when I saw what happened, I deeply and completely accept myself anyway...Even though I was frightened by what I saw, I choose to feel calm and peaceful now...Even though the fear from what I witnessed is still showing up in my eyes, I deeply and profoundly love and accept myself anyway.

Then tap on the following points while saying the phrases listed below:

EYEBROW: *I have this fear stuck in my eyes*

SIDE OF EYE: *I still feel afraid when I remember what I saw*

UNDER EYE: *I didn't want to see that*

UNDER NOSE: *No wonder I have been clouding my vision*

CHIN: *I wish I hadn't seen what I saw*

COLLARBONE: *This fear is stuck in my eyesight*

UNDER ARM: *The fear from that incident is stuck in my eyes*

HEAD: *I can't forget what I saw*

Then start tapping again on the eyebrow point and repeat these positive phrases:

EYEBROW: *What if I could resolve these feelings?*

SIDE OF EYE: *What if I could clear up my vision now?*

UNDER EYE: *I can get over what I saw*

UNDER NOSE: *I can forgive myself for looking*

CHIN: *I will forgive them for making me see that*

COLLARBONE: *I love allowing more clarity into my life*

UNDER ARM: *I appreciate my eyesight and my eyes*

HEAD: *I am grateful for the clarity in my life*

EFT ROUND #2

While tapping on the karate chop point, repeat the following phrases:

Even though I'm afraid to see more clearly, I accept who I am and how I have been behaving...Even though I am afraid to see more of what's out there, I choose to accept all of me and what I have done to my eyes...Even though the fear is stuck in my eyes, I choose to release the fear

Then tap on the following points while saying the phrases listed below:

EYEBROW: *I am afraid to see perfectly clearly*

SIDE OF EYE: *I am surprised at how strong the fear is*

UNDER EYE: *If I see too clearly, I might see more of what I saw back then*

UNDER NOSE: *Sometimes it's not good to see so much*

CHIN: *I will never forget what I saw*

COLLARBONE: *This resistance to clearing up my vision*

UNDER ARM: *I have so much fear in my eyesight*

HEAD: *I am so afraid to see clearly again*

Then start tapping again on the eyebrow point and repeat these positive phrases:

EYEBROW: *I choose to release the fear*

SIDE OF EYE: *It was a long time ago*

UNDER EYE: *I choose to feel ready to release all the fear from my eyes*

UNDER NOSE: *I feel free to release the fear right now*

CHIN: *I choose to see whatever I want*

COLLARBONE: *It feels so good to allow myself to see clearly again*

UNDER ARM: *I appreciate my eyesight and my eyes*

HEAD: *I am grateful for my improving vision*

EFT ROUND #3

While tapping on the karate chop point, repeat the following phrases:

Even though I am afraid to release this fear, I choose to feel calm and peaceful now...Even though I have been frightened for so long because of what happened, I accept who I am and how I dealt with what I saw...Even though this fear has been with me for years, hiding in my eyesight, I accept myself and love myself and my eyes anyway.

Then tap on the following points while saying the phrases listed below:

EYEBROW: *I'm afraid I'll see something bad again like last time*

SIDE OF EYE: *I don't want to see something bad again*

UNDER EYE: *I am afraid to see what's in front of me*

UNDER NOSE: *I'm afraid to see clearly*

CHIN: *I don't really want to see more clearly*

COLLARBONE: *I don't feel safe seeing more clearly*

UNDER ARM: *This resistance to improving my eyesight is all about fear*

HEAD: *I remember what I saw, no wonder I don't want to clear up my vision*

Then start tapping again on the eyebrow point and repeat these positive phrases:

EYEBROW: *I can release the fear from what I saw*

SIDE OF EYE: *I managed to survive anyway*

UNDER EYE: *I appreciate feeling so strong even though it was scary*

UNDER NOSE: *I feel free to release the fear from my eyes*

CHIN: *I choose to let go of this fear in my eyes and eyesight*

COLLARBONE: *I choose to allow clarity into my life*

UNDER ARM: *I love the strength of my eyesight and my eyes*

HEAD: *I appreciate the clarity in my life*

EFT
EYESIGHT
EXPERIMENT

WEEK #2

"Reminder"

I am getting some wonderful success stories after the end of week #1... This is from a participant:

"...After 3 days I realized that for the first time I was seeing some colors in my neighbor's house that I never have seen before. Also I had a burning pain in my left eye when I was doing the exercises that is now gone, my eyes were very dry and it is also almost gone..."

What this confirms is that our emotions are showing up in our eyesight. Keep up the tapping.

Use the **EFT recommendations** every day for at least 5 minutes. *Make sure you complete 7 days of week #1's exercises before moving on.*

For those of you who can't see/read the written phrases without your corrective lenses, *go ahead and wear them while you tap!!* Or make the written suggestions into a huge point size on your computer for easier viewing.

But your before and after eye "test" must be performed without them.

Sometimes when you tap on heavy emotional issues, the problem (your eyesight) might get temporarily worse before it gets better. Don't worry about this, keep tapping on the emotions that are in your eyes...

For those of you who are not familiar with **EFT**, please go to **www. emofree.com** for the free downloadable manual or the excellent tutorial program. As I made clear in my original instructions, **I am unable to answer any personal emails about the experiment or any questions about the basics of the EFT process**.

Thank you,

Carol Look

WEEK #3

GUILT

EFT
EYESIGHT
EXPERIMENT

WEEK #3

Remember that you all agreed to take full responsibility for yourself and your emotional and physical well-being when you signed up for this experiment.

That means if you are having any medical issues related to your eyes, you are expected to seek medical attention immediately...

FROM ANOTHER PARTICIPANT:

"I have been doing the improving eyesight exercises and in one week, the dryness problem I had and was about to see a Dr. about is almost completely alleviated!!! Also, the "seeing more clearly" seems to be helping me "see" certain situations and people I have been struggling with lately about my divorce etc., more clearly. Thanks, thanks, thanks..."

MAKE SURE YOU COMPLETE 7 DAYS OF TAPPING BEFORE MOVING ON TO INSTRUCTIONS FOR THE FOLLOWING WEEK.

Having questions about the basics of EFT? Go to www.emofree.com **for the free downloadable manual or the excellent tutorial program.**

ASSIGNMENTS

Print out each week's instructions and use them in a private, quiet place for **at least 5 minutes a day**.

For those of you who *can't read the statements without your glasses on*, by all means, wear your glasses!! Some participants are printing out the assignments in huge point sizes to take care of this problem. *However, the before and after eye "test" must be done without any corrective lenses on.*

Please keep exact records and fill in the questionnaire with the number of days per week you completed the assignments, and whether any eyesight measurements listed on the **questionnaire** changed or not from week to week.

Are you registering the improvements cumulatively, so that by the end of week #8, the number in the final box will represent your *total improvement* throughout the experiment? This is critical!

(For instance, if your a *ability to see color contrasts* seemed approximately 10% clearer after week #1, you would assign it a value of "1" in the box provided. If during week #2, you haven't noticed any more improvement, and you remain at a 10% improvement overall, you would assign that box a value of "1" again for the second week. If during week #3, you notice that overall you are at a 20% improvement, you will assign that box a value of "2" representing the cumulative 20% improvement.)

Remember to fill out your questionnaire before beginning the next 7 days.

Thanks, and enjoy it.

Carol Look

EFT
EYESIGHT
EXPERIMENT

WEEK #3:
GUILT

Choose 2 incidents from your past about which you feel guilty (something you said, did, or didn't say or didn't do!) Rate them on a scale of 0-10, then tap along and notice any improvements.

EFT ROUND #1

While tapping on the karate chop point, repeat the following phrases:

Even though I feel so guilty about what I did, I choose to accept and forgive myself now...Even though I have been punishing myself because of feeling guilty, I choose to release the guilt now...Even though the guilt has been trapped in my eyes, I have decided to accept myself and move on.

Then tap on the following points while saying the phrases listed below:

EYEBROW: *I feel this overwhelming guilt about what I did*

SIDE OF EYE: *I feel deeply guilty about what happened*

UNDER EYE: *I totally blame myself for what happened*

UNDER NOSE: *I don't deserve to be forgiven*

CHIN: *I don't really think I should forgive myself*

COLLARBONE: *I think I should continue to feel guilty*

UNDER ARM: *I don't want to forgive myself*

HEAD: *I'm not ready to forgive myself*

Then start tapping again on the eyebrow point and repeat these positive phrases:

EYEBROW: *I will consider releasing this old guilt*

SIDE OF EYE: *I would forgive someone else if they did what I did*

UNDER EYE: *I choose to release the guilt about what I did (said)*

UNDER NOSE: *I can allow myself to be forgiven*

CHIN: *I choose to release this old guilt*

COLLARBONE: *It's time to forgive myself*

UNDER ARM: *I release the guilt now*

HEAD: *I can see clearer already*

EFT ROUND #2

While tapping on the karate chop point, repeat the following phrases:

Even though I am still feeling guilty about what I said (or didn't say), I choose to accept and forgive myself now...Even though I'm holding onto this guilt for the wrong reasons, I choose to release it and forgive myself now...Even though I've been holding the guilt in my eyes, I feel ready to allow myself to see clearly again.

Then tap on the following points while saying the phrases listed below:

EYEBROW: *I've been punishing myself by clouding my vision*

SIDE OF EYE: *I've been holding the guilt in my eyesight*

UNDER EYE: *No wonder I have eyesight problems*

UNDER NOSE: *I thought it was the right thing to do to punish myself*

CHIN: *I keep wanting to hold onto the guilt*

COLLARBONE: *This resistance to forgiving myself*

UNDER ARM: *I would forgive someone else, but not me*

HEAD: *I'm not worthy of forgiveness*

Then start tapping again on the eyebrow point and repeat these positive phrases:

EYEBROW: *I will consider releasing the guilt*

SIDE OF EYE: *What if I am worthy of being forgiven?*

UNDER EYE: *What if it's time to forgive myself?*

UNDER NOSE: *What if it's time to let go of what happened?*

CHIN: *I choose to let go of all my guilt*

COLLARBONE: *I allow myself to let go of all my guilt*

UNDER ARM: *I learned enough from it and it's time to let go*

HEAD: *I am grateful for the new clarity in my vision*

EFT ROUND #3

While tapping on the karate chop point, repeat the following phrases:

Even though I feel deeply guilty about what I did, it's time to release it and forgive myself...Even though I am resistant to forgiving myself, I choose to forgive the others that were involved...Even though I still feel this incredible guilt, I am going to allow myself to forgive myself for being immature, insecure, and foolish.

Then tap on the following points while saying the phrases listed below:

EYEBROW: *Remaining guilt about what I did*

SIDE OF EYE: *I've been storing the guilt in my eyes*

UNDER EYE: *I am afraid to release the guilt*

UNDER NOSE: *I don't want to forgive myself*

CHIN: *I don't really think I deserve to be forgiven*

COLLARBONE: *I am resistant to forgiving myself*

UNDER ARM: *This resistance to forgiving myself and moving on*

HEAD: *The guilt is so strong*

Then start tapping again on the eyebrow point and repeat these positive phrases:

EYEBROW: *I will consider releasing the guilt*

SIDE OF EYE: *I am relieved I am turning the corner*

UNDER EYE: *I choose to feel ready to forgive myself*

UNDER NOSE: *I can feel myself releasing the guilt*

CHIN: *It feels so good to release the guilt*

COLLARBONE: *It feels so good to finally let go of what happened*

UNDER ARM: *I appreciate my eyesight and my eyes*

HEAD: *I am grateful for the clarity in my life*

EFT
EYESIGHT
EXPERIMENT

WEEK #3

"Reminder"

You all should be tapping with the recommendations for week #3. Remember to go to a quiet, private place before doing your tapping.

I continue to get some interesting and wonderful success stories from week to week... This is from another participant:

"After two weeks into the vision experiment, I am now able to read music at the piano without my glasses. (1.75 magnification) The telephone book is next...(2.75 magnification)"

Again, what this confirms is that our emotions are showing up in our eyesight. Keep up the tapping.

For those of you who can't see/read the written phrases without your corrective lenses, *go ahead and wear them while you tap!!* Or convert the written suggestions into a huge point size on your computer for easier viewing.

But your before and after eye "test" must be performed without them.

Sometimes when you tap on heavy emotional issues, the problem (your eyesight) might get temporarily worse before it gets better. Don't worry about this, keep tapping on the emotions that are in your eyes...

Don't forget to fill out your questionnaire, and measure the improvements cumulatively, so that at the end of week #3, the number in the box represents the total improvement so far.

Thank you,

Carol Look

WEEK #4

ANGER

(Parts 1 & 2)

EFT
EYESIGHT
EXPERIMENT

WEEK #4

Remember that you all agreed to take full responsibility for yourself and your emotional and physical well-being when you signed up for this experiment.

That means if you are having any medical issues related to your eyes, you are expected to seek medical attention immediately...

MAKE SURE YOU COMPLETE 7 DAYS OF TAPPING BEFORE MOVING ON TO INSTRUCTIONS FOR THE FOLLOWING WEEK.

ASSIGNMENTS

Print out each week's instructions and use them in a private, quiet place for **at least 5 minutes a day**.

For those of you who *can't read the statements without your glasses on*, by all means, wear your glasses!! Some participants are printing out the assignments in huge point sizes to take care of this problem. *However, the before and after eye "test" must be done without any corrective lenses on.*

Please keep exact records and fill in the questionnaire with the number of days per week you completed the assignments, and whether any eyesight measurements listed on the **questionnaire** changed or not from week to week.

Are you registering the improvements cumulatively, so that by the end of week #8, the number in the final box will represent your *total improvement* throughout the experiment? This is critical!

Thanks, and enjoy it.

Carol Look

EFT
EYESIGHT
EXPERIMENT

WEEK #4:
ANGER

Choose 2 incidents/people you feel extremely angry about. For your own purposes, rate your anger on a scale from 0-10. Tap on these incidents (people) separately, and note if the anger subsides and if there are any improvements in your eyesight.

(Remember, you should be doing the exercises **WITHOUT** any corrective lenses on.)

EFT ROUND #1

While tapping on the karate chop point, repeat the following phrases:

Even though I feel so angry about what happened, I deeply and completely love and accept myself...Even though I have felt angry for so long, I choose to accept myself and my feelings...Even though I feel entitled to still feel angry, I accept and love all of me anyway.

Then tap on the following points while saying the phrases listed below:

EYEBROW: *I feel so angry about what happened*

SIDE OF EYE: *The anger is in my eyesight*

UNDER EYE: *I still feel angry about what happened*

UNDER NOSE: *I can't let it go*

CHIN: *I don't want to let it go*

COLLARBONE: *This resistance to letting my anger go*

UNDER ARM: *I think I should hold onto my anger*

HEAD: *I have this need to stay angry*

Then start tapping again on the eyebrow point and repeat these positive phrases:

EYEBROW: *I will consider releasing the anger*

SIDE OF EYE: *No I won't*

UNDER EYE: *Yes I will*

UNDER NOSE: *I can let the anger go after all these years*

CHIN: *I choose to release the anger that I've been storing in my eyes*

COLLARBONE: *It feels so good to allow the anger to melt away*

UNDER ARM: *I choose to release the anger*

HEAD: *I am grateful that I can move on now*

EFT ROUND #2

While tapping on the karate chop point, repeat the following phrases:

Even though it doesn't feel safe releasing this old anger, I choose to feel confident about my feelings...Even though it doesn't feel right to forgive anyone involved, I accept and love myself anyway...Even though it feels safer to hold onto my anger, I accept and respect all of me now.

Then tap on the following points while saying the phrases listed below:

EYEBROW: *I still feel angry*

SIDE OF EYE: *I don't want to let go of my anger*

UNDER EYE: *Who will I be without my anger?*

UNDER NOSE: *It doesn't feel safe to release my anger*

CHIN: *I don't care if the anger is stored in my eyes*

COLLARBONE: *I refuse to let go of my anger*

UNDER ARM: *I have this resistance to releasing the anger*

HEAD: *I don't feel safe letting go of my anger*

Then start tapping again on the eyebrow point and repeat these positive phrases:

EYEBROW: *I will consider releasing some of my anger*

SIDE OF EYE: *What if I will feel safer releasing the anger?*

UNDER EYE: *I choose to feel ready to release the anger*

UNDER NOSE: *I will consider forgiving myself for holding on for so long*

CHIN: *I choose to feel safe now even if I let go of my anger*

COLLARBONE: *It feels so good to allow myself to release the anger*

UNDER ARM: *I appreciate my ability to release the anger*

HEAD: *I am grateful for my eyesight and am ready to let go of the anger*

EFT ROUND #3

While tapping on the karate chop point, repeat the following phrases:

Even though I am still so angry and can't imagine resolving this issue, I deeply and completely love and accept myself anyway... Even though I don't really want to release all my anger, who would I be without it, I choose to accept myself anyway...Even though I'm afraid to let go of my anger and see more clearly, I accept and love all of me.

Then tap on the following points while saying the phrases listed below:

EYEBROW: *It doesn't feel fair to let go of my anger*

SIDE OF EYE: *Shouldn't I remain angry?*

UNDER EYE: *What she/he did was wrong*

UNDER NOSE: *I don't want to let it go*

CHIN: *But I know it is blocking my vision*

COLLARBONE: *This blinding rage needs to be released*

UNDER ARM: *I am afraid to release my rage and anger*

HEAD: *I can't help this resistance to releasing the anger at them*

Then start tapping again on the eyebrow point and repeat these positive phrases:

EYEBROW: *I am ready to forgive myself*

SIDE OF EYE: *I will consider forgiving him/her*

UNDER EYE: *I choose to feel ready to release this stored anger*

UNDER NOSE: *I feel free to release the anger in my eyes*

CHIN: *I choose to feel free of the anger*

COLLARBONE: *It feels so good to allow clarity into my eyesight*

UNDER ARM: *I appreciate my eyesight and my eyes*

HEAD: *I am grateful for the freedom I feel right now*

EXPANDED SECTION
ON
ANGER

ANGER IN MY EYES, PART 2

The final results of the **EFT Eyesight Experiment** revealed that 42% of the respondents reported that stored anger had been negatively affecting their eyesight, and when they released some of it through the suggested **EFT** exercises, they noticed more pronounced changes in their vision. So I am including an expanded section on anger with an additional 3 rounds of **EFT**.

Again, you may choose incidents, events, or people you feel angry toward, scale the feelings on the 0-10 point scale, and then start tapping with the **EFT** rounds below.

EFT ROUND #1

While tapping on the karate chop point, repeat the following phrases:

Even though I feel angry and enraged about what they did to me, I deeply and completely love and accept myself anyway...Even though I have always felt angry about this, I choose to accept myself and my feelings...Even though I feel the need to stay angry, I accept and love who I am and how I feel anyway.

Then tap on the following points while saying the phrases listed below:

EYEBROW: *I feel extremely angry about what happened*

SIDE OF EYE: *The anger is stuck in my eyes*

UNDER EYE: *I still feel rage when I think about what happened*

UNDER NOSE: *I shouldn't let it go*

CHIN: *I don't want to let it go*

COLLARBONE: *I am furious*

UNDER ARM: *I am entitled to be furious*

HEAD: *I can feel the rage in my entire body*

Then start tapping again on the eyebrow point and repeat these positive phrases:

EYEBROW: *I might consider letting go of this blinding anger*

SIDE OF EYE: *No I won't*

UNDER EYE: *Yes I will*

UNDER NOSE: *I will let the anger go after all these years*

CHIN: *I choose to release the anger that I've been holding in my eyes*

COLLARBONE: *I choose to release my anger and rage*

UNDER ARM: *I choose to feel calm about what happened*

HEAD: *I feel peaceful and choose to move on now*

EFT ROUND #2

While tapping on the karate chop point, repeat the following phrases:

Even though it seems stupid and unsafe releasing this anger about what happened, I choose to feel accepting of all of me and my feelings...Even though it doesn't feel right to forgive anyone for what they did, I deeply and completely love and accept myself anyway...Even though it feels safe to stay angry at them, I accept and respect all of me now.

Then tap on the following points while saying the phrases listed below:

EYEBROW: *I still feel so angry about what happened*

SIDE OF EYE: *I refuse to let go of my anger*

UNDER EYE: *Who will I be without my anger?*

UNDER NOSE: *I refuse to release the rage from my eyes*

CHIN: *I don't care if the anger is stored in my eyes*

COLLARBONE: *It's not safe to let go of my anger*

UNDER ARM: *This resistance to releasing the anger*

HEAD: *I don't feel safe unless I feel angry*

Then start tapping again on the eyebrow point and repeat these positive phrases:

EYEBROW: *I could release some of my anger after all these years*

SIDE OF EYE: *What if I will feel safe even without my anger?*

UNDER EYE: *I choose to feel open to releasing some of the anger*

UNDER NOSE: *I will consider forgiving myself and them*

CHIN: *I choose to feel safe now even if I let go of my anger*

COLLARBONE: *I allow myself to let go of this anger*

UNDER ARM: *I appreciate who I am and why I needed to hold on*

HEAD: *I am grateful for my eyesight and am ready to let go of the anger*

EFT ROUND #3

While tapping on the karate chop point, repeat the following phrases:

Even though I am still enraged about this issue, I deeply and completely love and accept myself anyway...Even though I am reluctant to release all my anger, it doesn't feel safe, I choose to accept myself and these strong feelings anyway...Even though I'm afraid to let go of my anger and see more clearly, I accept and love all of me right now.

Then tap on the following points while saying the phrases listed below:

    EYEBROW: *Why should I let go of my anger?*

    SIDE OF EYE: *I need to stay angry about what happened*

    UNDER EYE: *What she/he did was wrong*

    UNDER NOSE: *I refuse to let it go*

    CHIN: *I wonder if it is blocking my vision*

    COLLARBONE: *This blinding rage in my eyes*

    UNDER ARM: *I'm not ready to release my rage and anger*

    HEAD: *I can't stop feeling angry at them*

Then start tapping again on the eyebrow point and repeat these positive phrases:

    EYEBROW: *I choose to forgive myself*

    SIDE OF EYE: *I will consider forgiving him/her*

    UNDER EYE: *I choose to feel ready to release the anger in my eyes*

    UNDER NOSE: *I feel free when I think of releasing this anger*

    CHIN: *I choose to feel free of the rage trapped in my eyesight*

COLLARBONE: *I have decided to allow clarity into my eyesight*

UNDER ARM: *I appreciate my eyesight and my eyes*

HEAD: *I am grateful for the freedom I feel right now*

WEEK #5

ANXIETY

EFT
EYESIGHT
EXPERIMENT

WEEK #5

FROM ANOTHER PARTICIPANT:

*"Thought you might want to hear the progress I'm experiencing already. The first week, I noticed a little more dryness and a little more clarity. The second week I think really hit home on the problem and it's funny, but it was at the exact time that I had a traumatic experience in my life (something a 5 year old should never have to see) that my eyesight started deteriorating. I didn't even put it all together until I was reading the assignment. So after doing assignment #2 for the whole week, **I am now noticing a lot of major changes.** Everything is just so bright, just so much brighter, I had to wear my sunglasses on a cloudy day just to give my eyes a break. So Amazing!!*

*When I first started I couldn't read the **E** from the distance I was suppose to set myself up to read (6.24 feet), so I wrote down that I could see the E with my heel at 62 inches. At the beginning of week #2, I could now read **E** and **F** with my heel at 62 inches. At the beginning of week 3, I can now read **EFLP**, truly amazing!! I also wrote down that in Week #1, I could read the 20/20 Line with my heel at 16 inches, at the beginning of week 2, I moved back to 17 inches and at the beginning of week 3, today, I can read the 20/20 line from 19 inches. I also checked what I can read from the 6.24 feet mark, and I can see the **E** - Hurray!! OK, that's about all for today, I just thought you'd appreciate getting some positive feedback."*

MAKE SURE YOU COMPLETE 7 DAYS OF TAPPING BEFORE MOVING ON TO INSTRUCTIONS FOR THE FOLLOWING WEEK.

ASSIGNMENTS

Print out each week's instructions and use them in a private, quiet place for **at least 5 minutes a day**.

For those of you who ***can't read the statements without your glasses on***, by all means, wear your glasses!! Some participants are printing out the assignments in huge point sizes to take care of this problem. ***However, the before and after eye "test" must be done without any corrective lenses on.***

Please keep exact records and fill in the questionnaire with the number of days per week you completed the assignments, and whether any eyesight measurements listed on the **questionnaire** changed or not from week to week.

Are you registering the improvements cumulatively, so that by the end of week #8, the number in the final box will represent your ***total improvement*** throughout the experiment? This is critical!

Thanks, and enjoy it.

Carol Look

EFT
EYESIGHT
EXPERIMENT

WEEK #5:
ANXIETY

Choose 2 incidents from your past, and 2 events coming up in your future. When you think of them, how high is your anxiety on a scale from 0-10? Rate them and tap along with these suggestions, monitoring the anxiety levels and your eyesight.

(Remember, you should be doing the exercises WITHOUT any corrective lenses on.)

EFT ROUND #1

While tapping on the karate chop point, repeat the following phrases:

Even though I've been holding all this anxiety in my eyes, I deeply and completely love and accept myself...Even though I have been storing anxiety in my vision, I choose to accept myself anyway...Even though I've been letting this anxiety from my past and about the future cloud my vision, I accept and love all of me no matter what.

Then tap on the following points while saying the phrases listed below:

EYEBROW: *I have so much anxiety in my eyes*

SIDE OF EYE: *I don't want to improve my eyesight*

UNDER EYE: *I am afraid to see more clearly*

UNDER NOSE: *The anxiety is stuck in my eyesight*

CHIN: *I don't really want to see more clearly*

COLLARBONE: *This resistance to clearing up my vision*

UNDER ARM: *I am afraid to release this anxiety*

HEAD: *So much anxiety clouding my vision*

Then start tapping again on the eyebrow point and repeat these positive phrases:

EYEBROW: *I will consider releasing the anxiety*

SIDE OF EYE: *I can allow myself to accept myself no matter what*

UNDER EYE: *I choose to feel accepting of this anxiety*

UNDER NOSE: *I feel free to release the anxiety now*

CHIN: *I allow myself to release the anxiety from my past*

COLLARBONE: *It feels so good to allow clarity into my life*

UNDER ARM: *I choose to feel so free and calm*

HEAD: *I am grateful that I can allow my vision to improve*

EFT ROUND #2

While tapping on the karate chop point, repeat the following phrases:

Even though I continue to store this anxiety in my eyesight, I deeply and completely love and accept myself...Even though I feel afraid of letting go of my anxiety, I choose to accept myself anyway...Even though all this anxiety has been in the way of seeing clearly, I choose to feel calm and peaceful and to accept and love all of me.

Then tap on the following points while saying the phrases listed below:

EYEBROW: *I continue to store anxiety in my eyes*

SIDE OF EYE: *I don't want to improve my eyesight*

UNDER EYE: *I am afraid to see more clearly*

UNDER NOSE: *I'm storing old anxiety in my vision problems*

CHIN: *This anxiety in my eyes*

COLLARBONE: *This resistance to clearing up my vision*

UNDER ARM: *This anxiety is trapped in my eyesight*

HEAD: *Remaining anxiety in my eyesight*

Then start tapping again on the eyebrow point and repeat these positive phrases:

EYEBROW: *I will consider releasing the old anxiety*

SIDE OF EYE: *I can allow myself to release the anxiety*

UNDER EYE: *I choose to feel calm and peaceful*

UNDER NOSE: *I choose to feel safe with clearer vision*

CHIN: *I choose to feel safe about the future*

COLLARBONE: *It feels so good to allow clarity into my life*

UNDER ARM: *I appreciate my eyesight and my eyes*

HEAD: *I am grateful for the clarity in my life*

EFT ROUND #3

While tapping on the karate chop point, repeat the following phrases:

Even though I have been blurring my vision with my anxiety, I deeply and completely love and accept myself anyway...Even though I didn't know I was hurting my eyes with the anxiety, I choose to completely forgive and accept myself anyway...Even though improving my vision makes me feel anxious, I accept and love all of me now.

Then tap on the following points while saying the phrases listed below:

EYEBROW: *I still have anxiety from my past*

SIDE OF EYE: *I still have anxiety about my future*

UNDER EYE: *A big part of me is afraid to see more clearly*

UNDER NOSE: *I thought I wanted to see better*

CHIN: *I don't really want to see better*

COLLARBONE: *This resistance to clearing up my vision*

UNDER ARM: *I have so much anxiety in my eyesight*

HEAD: *I have so much anxiety throughout my whole body*

Then start tapping again on the eyebrow point and repeat these positive phrases:

EYEBROW: *I choose to feel calm and peaceful*

SIDE OF EYE: *I can allow myself to feel calm and peaceful*

UNDER EYE: *I choose to feel ready to release the past anxiety*

UNDER NOSE: *I feel free to release the anxiety about my future*

CHIN: *I choose to feel free, calm, and peaceful*

COLLARBONE: *It feels so good to allow clarity into my life*

UNDER ARM: *I appreciate my eyesight and my eyes*

HEAD: *I am grateful for my crystal clear eyesight*

WEEK #6

BELIEFS
ABOUT AGING

EFT
EYESIGHT
EXPERIMENT

WEEK #6

FROM ANOTHER PARTICIPANT:

"...at the end of Week 4, I did my own self-test with the eye chart on the computer screen. After doing my last round of tapping for Sunday, I went immediately to the computer Eye Chart, put my chair back the appropriate amount, and wrote down the letters I could see - both eyes together, only the left and then only the right. Then I went back to my notes about what these letters had been before starting Week 1. I hadn't done this comparison before and was I ever excited! My left eye had gone from 20/100 to 20/40, and my right eye went from 20/100 to 20/30 (NO glasses). I didn't even know there was a 20/20 line on the chart when I started. Was I ever jazzed!

My goal of course is to throw away my glasses - I've been wearing them since I was 2 years old - so I guess you could say 'all my life'. At first I didn't want to be overly optimistic that this would work and then be disappointed. But as I've progressed in this experiment and as I've continued to watch Gary Craig's Palace of Possibilities, I said 'what the heck - go for the GOLD!'

Thank you for all your effort that you have put into this rewarding experience. You have given me hope."

MAKE SURE YOU COMPLETE 7 DAYS OF TAPPING BEFORE MOVING ON TO INSTRUCTIONS FOR THE FOLLOWING WEEK.

EFT EYESIGHT EXPERIMENT

WEEK #6:

BELIEFS ABOUT AGING/ SPECIFIC PROBLEMS

(Remember, you should be doing the exercises WITHOUT any corrective lenses on, unless you can't read the suggestions without them!)

<u>EFT ROUND #1</u>

While tapping on the karate chop point, repeat the following phrases:

Even though I am convinced that we all develop eyesight problems as we age, I deeply and completely love and accept myself...Even though everyone has to have eye problems as they age, I choose to accept myself anyway...Even though I don't believe that I can improve my eyesight because I'm getting older, I accept and love all of me, my eyes, and my body.

Then tap on the following points while saying the phrases listed below:

EYEBROW: *I am convinced everyone has eyesight problems because of aging*

SIDE OF EYE: *Doesn't everyone have eye problems as they age?*

UNDER EYE: *I was taught that my problems were due to getting older*

UNDER NOSE: *I thought everyone knew this*

CHIN: *Isn't this the truth?*

COLLARBONE: *It didn't occur to me that my emotions were causing the problems*

UNDER ARM: *These emotions in my eyesight*

HEAD: *What if it isn't true...*

Then start tapping again on the eyebrow point and repeat these positive phrases:

EYEBROW: *I will consider that my age is not connected to my eye problems*

SIDE OF EYE: *I wonder if it's possible to regain perfect vision*

UNDER EYE: *I can't believe all my limiting beliefs*

UNDER NOSE: *I just assumed they were true*

CHIN: *What if I can improve my eyesight no matter how old I am?*

COLLARBONE: *I feel so free all of a sudden*

UNDER ARM: *I appreciate my eyesight and am ready to make it stronger*

HEAD: *I am ready to release these old beliefs*

EFT ROUND #2

While tapping on the karate chop point, repeat the following phrases:

Even though I have this _____ (astigmatism, cloudiness, cataracts, macular degeneration, floaters, nearsightedness, far sightedness etc...) in my eye(s), I deeply and completely love and accept myself anyway...Even though I have had this problem for years, and a part of me doesn't really want to improve my vision, I choose to accept myself anyway...Even though I'm afraid to see more clearly, and that's why I developed _____, I deeply and completely love and accept all of me.

Then tap on the following points while saying the phrases listed below:

EYEBROW: *I have this _____ (your particular problem)*

SIDE OF EYE: *This _____*

UNDER EYE: *I'm not sure I want to get over it*

UNDER NOSE: *I am afraid to see more clearly*

CHIN: *I can see how it has helped me hide from something*

COLLARBONE: *I still have this _____ in my eyes*

UNDER ARM: *This _____ in my eyes*

HEAD: *I thought it was hereditary, that's what they told me*

Then start tapping again on the eyebrow point and repeat these positive phrases:

EYEBROW: *I will consider releasing this problem I've had for so long*

SIDE OF EYE: *I can allow myself to let go of this _____*

UNDER EYE: *I choose to feel ready to release this _____*

UNDER NOSE: *I feel free to release this _____ in my eyes*

CHIN: *I am letting go right now*

COLLARBONE: *It feels so good to know these new truths*

UNDER ARM: *I appreciate my eyesight*

HEAD: *I am grateful that I know I can improve my vision*

EFT ROUND #3

While tapping on the karate chop point, repeat the following phrases:

Even though I am still convinced some of my problems come from my age and my ancestors, I deeply and completely love and accept myself... Even though I am afraid to let go of some of these limiting beliefs about aging and my eyesight, I choose to accept myself anyway...Even though I'm afraid to see more clearly, that's why I am hanging on to these beliefs, I deeply and completely respect, accept and love all of me.

Then tap on the following points while saying the phrases listed below:

EYEBROW: *I still have some resistance to improving my eyesight*

SIDE OF EYE: *I don't want to improve my eyesight*

UNDER EYE: *I am afraid to see more clearly*

UNDER NOSE: *Don't we all have vision problems because of aging?*

CHIN: *Don't we all have eyesight problems that were passed down to us?*

COLLARBONE: *Maybe they only passed down beliefs to me*

UNDER ARM: *Maybe it's time to release these limiting beliefs*

HEAD: *I am at least willing to consider improving my eyesight now*

Then start tapping again on the eyebrow point and repeat these positive phrases:

EYEBROW: *I will consider clearing up these problems in my eyes*

SIDE OF EYE: *I choose to allow myself to see more clearly*

UNDER EYE: *I so appreciate the clarity in my life*

UNDER NOSE: *I feel free to be open to incoming guidance*

CHIN: *I choose to let go of this resistance to improving my eyesight*

COLLARBONE: *It feels so good to allow clarity into my life*

UNDER ARM: *I appreciate my eyesight and how good it has been*

HEAD: *Thank you Universe (God, Spirit, Higher Power...or whatever) for bringing me clear vision*

WEEK #7

RESENTMENT
&
HURT

EFT
EYESIGHT
EXPERIMENT

WEEK #7

FROM ANOTHER PARTICIPANT:

"My problem is farsightedness, and I thought my near vision had been getting a tiny bit better during these weeks, but it was so subtle I was uncertain.

This week I reached a measurable milestone: I had started out needing to wear my glasses to read your tapping instructions. Yesterday I realized I can read them unaided now! I even went back to the week 1 and week 2 printouts to make sure it's not due to possible font size differences. It's not, I can read those same printouts without glasses now. I'm amazed and psyched. Thank you so much!"

MAKE SURE YOU COMPLETE 7 DAYS OF TAPPING BEFORE MOVING ON TO INSTRUCTIONS FOR THE FOLLOWING WEEK.

ASSIGNMENTS

Print out each week's instructions and use them in a private, quiet place for **at least 5 minutes a day.**

Please keep exact records and fill in the questionnaire…

Are you registering the improvements cumulatively, so that by the end of week #8, the number in the final box will represent your *total improvement* throughout the experiment? This is critical!

Thanks, and enjoy it.

Carol Look

EFT
EYESIGHT
EXPERIMENT

WEEK #7:
RESENTMENT & HURT

Choose 1 or 2 incidents about which you feel deeply resentful or hurt. Do they still "sting" when you think about them? Scale the feelings from 0-10, and tap along with the following phrases.

While tapping on the karate chop point, repeat the following phrases:

Even though I feel so resentful about what happened, I deeply and completely love and accept myself...Even though I can't seem to release this resentment, I choose to accept myself anyway...Even though I'm afraid to let go of the resentment and see more clearly, I accept and love all of me just as I am.

Then tap on the following points while saying the phrases listed below:

EYEBROW: *I have this resentment in my eyes*

SIDE OF EYE: *I don't want to let go of the resentment*

UNDER EYE: *I am afraid to see the situation clearly*

UNDER NOSE: *I don't want to forgive them*

CHIN: *I still feel resentful about what happened*

COLLARBONE: *This resistance to releasing resentment*

UNDER ARM: *The resentment is clouding my vision*

HEAD: *I can't help this resentment*

Then start tapping again on the eyebrow point and repeat these positive phrases:

EYEBROW: *I will consider releasing the resentment*

SIDE OF EYE: *I've been holding onto it for so many years*

UNDER EYE: *It doesn't feel safe to release it*

UNDER NOSE: *Yes it does*

CHIN: *I choose to let go of this resentment and resistance*

COLLARBONE: *My resentment hasn't helped the situation*

UNDER ARM: *I haven't considered letting it go until now*

HEAD: *I am grateful that I feel free to release the resentment now*

EFT ROUND #2

While tapping on the karate chop point, repeat the following phrases:

Even though I still feel hurt because of what he/she said, I deeply and completely love and accept myself...Even though I remember it as if it happened yesterday, I choose to accept myself anyway...Even though I'm afraid to see more clearly about this situation, I accept and love all of me just the way I am.

Then tap on the following points while saying the phrases listed below:

EYEBROW: *I have this hurt buried in my eyesight*

SIDE OF EYE: *I don't want to improve my eyesight*

UNDER EYE: *I am afraid to release the hurt*

UNDER NOSE: *I thought the hurt protected me*

CHIN: *I don't really want to see what happened back then*

COLLARBONE: *This resistance to releasing the hurt*

UNDER ARM: *I still feel hurt when I think about what happened*

HEAD: *I can't help these hurt feelings*

Then start tapping again on the eyebrow point and repeat these positive phrases:

EYEBROW: *I will consider releasing the hurt*

SIDE OF EYE: *I am allowing myself to release the hurt*

UNDER EYE: *I choose to feel ready to release the hurt*

UNDER NOSE: *I feel free to release the hurt in my eyesight*

CHIN: *I choose to let go of this hurt in my eyesight*

COLLARBONE: *It feels so good to allow clarity back into my eyesight*

UNDER ARM: *I appreciate all of me*

HEAD: *I am grateful for the new clarity in my life*

EFT ROUND #3

While tapping on the karate chop point, repeat the following phrases:

Even though I have been letting the old resentment and hurt cloud my vision, I deeply and completely love and accept myself...Even though I don't really want to let go of this hurt and resentment, I choose to accept myself anyway...Even though I'm afraid to see more clearly, it doesn't feel safe to release these feelings, I deeply and completely accept and love all of me.

Then tap on the following points while saying the phrases listed below:

EYEBROW: *I am holding onto so much resistance in my eyes*

SIDE OF EYE: *This hurt in my eyes*

UNDER EYE: *I'm holding the hurt in my eyes*

UNDER NOSE: *The hurt is blurring my vision*

CHIN: *I don't really want to see more clearly*

COLLARBONE: *I'm not ready to forgive them yet*

UNDER ARM: *I refuse to release the hurt and resentment*

HEAD: *I can't help wanting to hold onto this hurt*

Then start tapping again on the eyebrow point and repeat these positive phrases:

EYEBROW: *I will consider forgiving them when I feel ready*

SIDE OF EYE: *I allow myself to release the resentment*

UNDER EYE: *I'm tired of resentment and feel free to release it*

UNDER NOSE: *I choose to feel free of the resentment and hurt*

CHIN: *I choose to let go of these feelings in my eyes*

COLLARBONE: *It feels so good to allow clarity back into my life*

UNDER ARM: *I appreciate my eyesight and my eyes*

HEAD: *I am deeply grateful for my clear vision*

WEEK #8

REMAINING BLOCKS

TO IMPROVING MY

EYESIGHT

EFT
EYESIGHT
EXPERIMENT

WEEK #8

<u>For most of you, this is your last week of exercises.</u>

MAKE SURE YOU COMPLETE 7 DAYS OF TAPPING BEFORE MOVING ON TO INSTRUCTIONS FOR THE FOLLOWING WEEK.

Please keep exact records and fill in the questionnaire with the number of days per week you completed the assignments, and whether any eyesight measurements listed on the **questionnaire** changed or not from week to week.

Are you registering the improvements cumulatively, so that by the end of week #8, the number in the final box will represent your *total improvement* throughout the experiment? This is critical!

You will be asked to input your data starting Monday. I will be sending you a link where you will answer questions and input your results. Stay tuned...

Thanks, and enjoy it.

Carol Look

EFT
EYESIGHT
EXPERIMENT

WEEK #8:
REMAINING BLOCKS to
IMPROVING MY EYESIGHT

Even when we have tapped and tapped, there might still be some "Yes, but's…" in our minds about why it might not be safe or good or enjoyable to release the conflicts behind our less than perfect vision. If you suspect there are other reasons you may not want to improve your eyesight, by all means, use those "reasons" as the subject for tapping. Otherwise, use what I have written below.

EFT ROUND #1

While tapping on the karate chop point, repeat the following phrases:

Even though I have some remaining blocks to clearing up my eyesight, I deeply and completely love and accept myself…Even though I am extremely stubborn and don't really want to improve my vision, I choose to accept myself anyway…Even though I'm afraid to see more clearly because it doesn't feel safe, no wonder I am holding onto my blocks, I accept and love all of me just as I am.

Then tap on the following points while saying the phrases listed below:

EYEBROW: *I have some stubborn remaining blocks*

SIDE OF EYE: *I don't want to improve my eyesight*

UNDER EYE: *I still don't feel safe seeing clearly*

UNDER NOSE: *I have these remaining blocks to clear vision*

CHIN: *I want to be ready to release the resistance and blocks*

COLLARBONE: *This resistance to clearing up my vision is no longer useful*

UNDER ARM: *I had this poor eyesight but I am moving on now*

HEAD: *I am grateful I can let it go once and for all*

Then start tapping again on the eyebrow point and repeat these positive phrases:

EYEBROW: *I will consider releasing the resistance*

SIDE OF EYE: *I am allowing myself to get over this resistance*

UNDER EYE: *I choose to feel ready to release the resistance*

UNDER NOSE: *I love feeling ready for exceptional vision*

CHIN: *I choose to let go of this resistance*

COLLARBONE: *It feels so good to allow clarity into my life*

UNDER ARM: *I appreciate my eyesight and my eyes*

HEAD: *I am grateful for the clarity in my life and I allow my eyes to improve now*

EFT ROUND #2

While tapping on the karate chop point, repeat the following phrases:

Even though there were some good reasons to be resistant to improving my eyesight, I deeply and completely love and accept myself...Even though I didn't really want to improve my vision, I choose to accept myself and allow the improvement into my life now...Even though I was afraid to see more clearly because it didn't feel safe, I accept and love all of me as I change now.

Then tap on the following points while saying the phrases listed below:

EYEBROW: *I had this resistance to improving my eyesight*

SIDE OF EYE: *I didn't want to improve my eyesight*

UNDER EYE: *I was afraid to see more clearly*

UNDER NOSE: *I thought I wanted to see better*

CHIN: *I didn't really want to see better*

COLLARBONE: *These remaining blocks to clearing up my vision*

UNDER ARM: *I had this resistance to improving my eyesight*

HEAD: *I am now ready to release the resistance once and for all*

Then start tapping again on the eyebrow point and repeat these positive phrases.

EYEBROW: *I love knowing I am ready now*

SIDE OF EYE: *I can allow myself to get over this resistance*

UNDER EYE: *I choose to feel ready to release any vision blocks*

UNDER NOSE: *I feel free to release any eye problems*

CHIN: *I choose to let go of this resistance*

COLLARBONE: *It feels so good to allow clarity into my life*

UNDER ARM: *I appreciate my eyesight and my eyes*

HEAD: *I am grateful for my excellent vision*

EFT ROUND #3

While tapping on the karate chop point, repeat the following phrases:

Even though I have been afraid to improve my eyesight, I deeply and completely love and accept myself...Even though I didn't really want to improve my vision, I choose to accept myself anyway...Even though I was afraid to see more clearly, I choose to allow my vision to clear up now.

Then tap on the following points while saying the phrases listed below:

EYEBROW: *I had this resistance to improving my eyesight*

SIDE OF EYE: *I was afraid to improve my eyesight*

UNDER EYE: *I didn't feel safe seeing more clearly*

UNDER NOSE: *I had good reasons to block my vision*

CHIN: *I accept myself for being afraid*

COLLARBONE: *This resistance is surprising to me still*

UNDER ARM: *I still have some resistance to improving my eyesight*

HEAD: *I am releasing this resistance now*

Then start tapping again on the eyebrow point and repeat these positive phrases:

EYEBROW: *I know I am finally ready to release this resistance*

SIDE OF EYE: *I am allowing myself to get over this resistance*

UNDER EYE: *I choose to feel ready to see clearly now*

UNDER NOSE: *I feel free to allow my vision to clear up*

CHIN: *I choose to be open to all that I see*

COLLARBONE: *It feels so good to allow clarity into my life*

UNDER ARM: *I choose to appreciate my eyesight and my eyes*

HEAD: *I am grateful for my exceptional vision*

EFT
EYESIGHT
EXPERIMENT

RESULTS QUESTIONNAIRE

Individuals who completed the eyesight experiment were invited to enter their results on the following form.

Please **complete all fields** before clicking on the "**Submit My Results**" button at the end of this form. *Thank you!*

Eyesight experiment feedback should be emailed to <u>Carol@CarolLook.com</u>.

Name:	
Email address:	
Gender:	Female Male
Age:	
Before the experiment information	
Eyesight checked in last 3 months?	Yes No
My beginning prescription is: *Specify the spherical diopter reading for each eye (R/L).*	Right (OD) *(Example: -5.25)* Left (OS)
I wear glasses:	Yes No
I wear contact lenses:	Yes No

I have had Lasik surgery:	Yes No
I have had other eye surgery *(please specify)*:	
Please report any relevant diagnosis from your doctor: *(glaucoma, macular degeneration, corneal issues, etc.)*	
Start Date: *(yyyy-mm-dd)*:	

Carefully complete the form below for each week of EFT eyesight exercises. Be sure that your ratings match the key below:

NA = Not applicable (no need for improvement)

0 = no change

1 = very little change/improvement (up to 15%)

2 = a slight improvement (15 - 25%)

3 = noticeable improvement (25 - 50%)

4 = definite improvement (50 - 75%)

5 = significant improvement (75% or more)

	Week 1	Week 2	Week 3	Week 4	Week 5	Week 6	Week 7	Week 8
Times/ week I used EFT Exercises								
Brightness								

Color Perception									
Color Contrast									
Dryness									
Clarity (near)									
Clarity (far)									
Eye Fatigue									
Eye Burning/ Itching									
Eye Strain									
Floaters (decrease)									

End Date: *(yyyy-mm-dd)*:	
Did you have your eyes checked before and after by a doctor or through the eyesight chart provided for you?	Doctor Eyesight chart Both
Ending prescription is: *(For those who had doctor's eye examinations before and after the experiment)*	Right (OD) *(Example: -5.25)* Left (OS)
Overall, how would you rate the improvement in your eyesight at the end of 8 weeks?	

Additional Questions

1. You were asked to tap on a variety of very strong emotions each week. When you worked on these emotions, which one seemed to cause the most dramatic changes in your eyesight (guilt, anxiety, anger, hurt)?

2. What was the biggest reason you might have been reluctant to improve your eyesight?

3. Were you surprised about feelings and incidents from childhood that surfaced?

4. Did you seek additional EFT help when these exercises triggered strong feelings?
   Yes   No

5. Were you ever tempted to drop out of the experiment?
   Yes   No

6. Were there other physical or emotional changes you noted as a result of doing these regular EFT exercises?

7. What was the most significant change for you as a result of the experiment in either your eyesight or your emotions?
   Eyesight   Emotion   Neither

Please explain:

8. Did your nearsightedness change at all?
   No change   Better   Worse

9. Did your farsightedness change at all?
   No change   Better   Worse

10. Would you recommend this experiment to your friends or family members?
    Absolutely! I'm thrilled with the results!

    Yes!

    Maybe

    No

WHAT NEXT?

Now that you have completed the official assignments for the ***EFT Eyesight Experiment***, I encourage you to review the topics that most resonated with you. Repeat these assignments daily, or until you are satisfied with your final results. Then consider incorporating **EFT** into your daily life for stress and challenges of any kind, and at a minimum, once a week for maintenance of your eyesight improvement.

In the event that you did not notice enough improvement in your eyesight, I highly recommend ***being more specific*** with your setup phrases about what events or feelings might be "caught" in your eyes. Review your history and relationships with family members, friends, and lovers, and tap for any conflicts that you identify.

You may also apply all of the setup statements and assignments in this book to other physical challenges such as hearing loss, pain, fatigue, etc. (Please note, however, that **EFT** is not meant to replace proper medical or emotional treatment.)

In my personal and professional experience, I have yet to find a healing tool as elegant and efficient as **EFT**. I encourage you to continue using **EFT** for your emotional well-being and physical health.

RESULTS

OF THE

<u>EFT</u>

<u>EYESIGHT</u>

<u>EXPERIMENT</u>

RESULTS
OF THE
EFT EYESIGHT EXPERIMENT

Designed and conducted by Carol Look

Data Analysis and editorial support
　　by Jayne Morgan-Kidd (<u>www.jaynemorgankidd.com</u>)
Final Data Questionnaire
　　by Rick Wilkes (<u>www.thrivingnow.com</u>)
Editorial support
　　by Dr. Patricia Carrington (<u>www.eftupdate.com</u>)

Preliminary Report by Carol Look

<u>**RESEARCH QUESTION**</u>: Is it possible for a person with a vision problem to improve their eyesight by using **Emotional Freedom Techniques (EFT)**?

Based on the results recorded below, the answer appears to be a resounding yes!!

<u>DESCRIPTION OF EMOTIONAL FREEDOM TECHNIQUES (EFT)</u>

EFT is a form of meridian therapy based on the ancient Chinese technique of acupuncture. The **EFT** practitioner taps on designated acupressure points while inviting the client to tune in to the emotion or problem that has been chosen for treatment.

THE PARTICIPANTS

Participants were volunteers recruited through announcements in Carol Look's newsletter and at energy psychology conferences. At the beginning of this experiment, over 400 people expressed interest in this study and chose to participate. All of them already knew **EFT**. During the course of the 8 weeks, all but 120 dropped out. Many thanks to these 120 who diligently tapped on the **EFT** setups and suggestions provided.

Most of the participants (82%) were women. Most participants (nearly 70%) had not had their eyesight tested during the 3 months prior to the beginning of the study.

Over 80% indicated that they wear glasses for vision correction. Twenty percent wear contact lenses.

Participants ranged in age from 30-80. The average age was 52, with just over half the participants in their 50's.

To read the Table below see section "How To Read The Tables"

AGE GROUPS

		Frequency	Percent	Valid Percent	Cumulative Percent
Valid	30's	10	8.3	8.5	8.5
	40's	27	22.5	22.9	31.4
	50's	62	51.7	**52.5**	83.9
	60's	16	13.3	13.6	97.5
	70's	2	1.7	1.7	99.2
	80's	1	.8	.8	100.0
	Total	118	98.3	100.0	
Missing	System	2	1.7		
Total		120	100.0		

Statistical tests were used to determine differences between various groups, such as gender and age. The following were found to be statistically significant (p<.05):

1) **There was a significant difference between men and women in terms of overall eyesight improvement** (p=.022) in that **women improved their eyesight more than men did.** (The test accounts for the difference in group size.)

2) Over 28% of the final respondents reported that they sought additional **EFT** help. **There was no significant difference between those who sought additional EFT help during the course of the experiment and those that did not** in terms of their overall eyesight improvement.

3) There were **no** statistically significant differences in age groups in terms of overall improvement in eyesight. **This is a curious finding, considering that the popular belief is that eyesight deterioration coincides with the aging process.**

STUDY DESIGN:

Each study participant was sent weekly emails with a topic for tapping. (Fear, anger, guilt, hurt, etc) Three full sets of **EFT** setup statements were written out for the participants, with each set followed by one **EFT** tapping round focusing on the problem, followed by a second round that focused on the possibility of a solution.

This eyesight experiment was made available primarily to people who were already familiar with **EFT**. Announcements were made at **EFT** conferences and through newsletters.

ANALYSIS

Data was analyzed using SPSS, a statistical software designed for the social sciences. T-tests and ANOVA's were used to detect significant differences in groups.

HOW TO READ THE TABLES

Example:

		Frequency	Percent	Valid Percent	Cumulative Percent
	Slight improvement (15-25%)	**25**	20.8	**20.8**	71.7
Missing	No response				

'**Frequency**' refers to how many participants chose this response. In this case, 25 people indicated a 'slight improvement'.

'**Percent**' is the percentage of total number of participants.

'**Valid percent**' excludes those who:

1) did not answer the question or
2) did not have the symptom addressed in that question.

'**Valid percent**' gives the clearest picture of the overall result.

'**Cumulative percent**' simply adds the percentages in each row cumulatively.

'**Missing**' or 'System missing' shows the number of people who did not answer that question.

RESULTS:

OVERALL EYESIGHT IMPROVEMENT:

As the table below indicates, nearly 75% of participants in this study indicated that an improvement occurred in their vision during and by the end of the study.

OVERALL Eyesight Improvement

Valid		Frequency	Percent	Valid Percent	Cumulative Percent
Valid	No change	31	25.8	25.8	25.8
	very little change (up to 15%)	30	25.0	**25.0**	50.8
	Slight improvement (15-25%)	25	20.8	**20.8**	71.7
	Noticeable improvement (25-50%)	18	15.0	**15.0**	86.7
	Definite improvement (50-75%)	8	6.7	**6.7**	93.3
	Significant improvement (over 75%)	8	6.7	**6.7**	100.0
	Total	120	100.0	100.0	

Only 25% indicated no change.

TEMPTED TO DROP OUT:

At the beginning of this study, over 400 people expressed interest and chose to participate. During the course of the 8 weeks, all but 120 dropped out. I received numerous emails informing me that participants could no longer continue as "life" was getting in the way. Reasons included ailing elderly parents, daily stress, the upcoming holiday season, being called out of town, and no longer being interested in the experiment. (I suspect that some people, if they did not notice significant improvement immediately, were no longer "held" by the experiment.)

In addition, I was unable to offer individualized coaching or counseling, and it is possible that *secondary gains* (advantages of maintaining poor eyesight) were more likely to retain a foothold without outside help. *Comfort zones* about what is possible with improving one's vision were definitely challenged by this experiment.

Slightly under half of the **participants (44%) that stayed in the study were 'tempted to drop out'** at some point, for example, one participant wrote in:

> *"I had a hard time with week 4 – anger. I do not seem to have a problem with anger. When something negative happens around me I will go to feeling sorry for somebody or feeling hurt about a situation, but not anger. As a life coach and self improvement junkie, I do not think that I am stuffing the anger. I really think I simply don't have a lot of anger. Thus, week 4 was difficult to tap on things like "this blinding rage needs to be released", etc. It seemed negative to be tapping on something that was not there. This was the week I was tempted to drop out of the experiment."*

Q5: Tempted to drop out

		Frequency	Percent	Valid Percent	Cumulative Percent
Valid	No	66	55.0	55.9	55.9
	Yes	52	43.3	**44.1**	100.0
	Total	118	98.3	100.0	
Missing	No response	2	1.7		
Total		120	100.0		

I asked the participants of the study to name their known diagnoses with regard to vision, even though we didn't target any particular medical diagnoses in the study. The most common diagnosis reported was Astigmatism, and over half of the participants did not report a diagnoses.

Diagnosis	Number of those reporting a diagnosis (% of those reporting a diagnosis)
Astigmatism	16 (29%)
Farsightedness	3 (5%)
Nearsightedness (short sightedness, myopia)	5 (9%)
Floaters	7 (13%)
Glaucoma	3 (5%)
Cataracts	5 (9%)
All others reported	16 (29%)
None reported	65 (not included in %)

TAPPING COMPLIANCE:

Participants were asked to use the **EFT** assignments once a day. Eighty-six percent of participants reported that they tapped 7 or more times at the end of week one of this experiment. At the end of the second week, the number of people tapping 7 or more times dropped slightly to about 82%. For the next 3 weeks, this trend held fairly well. During the last 3 weeks, the number of people who reported tapping 7 or more time dropped again to mid to lower 70% range. Most people in this study complied well with the instructions.

FINAL QUESTIONNAIRE:

In the final questionnaire, participants were asked to answer certain questions about their emotions and responses to the experiment in addition to tabulating their numeric results. Some of the questions and answers are as follows:

Q1: Which emotion you tapped on caused the most dramatic changes in your eyesight?

Anger was mentioned 42 times, far more often than any other emotion. Also of interest was the fact that 3 people indicated that their most dramatic response was during the tapping sessions on beliefs about aging. (If this question had included this limiting belief as one of the choices, there may well have been more response in this area.)

Emotion	Number of times mentioned
Anger	**42**
Anxiety	24
Fear	20
Guilt	21

Hurt	19	
All	3	
None	14	

Q2: What was the biggest reason you might have been reluctant to improve your eyesight?

Although there was a variety of responses, **three repetitive themes emerged** throughout this section:

1) Fear of memories that could surface or **fear of *'seeing'*** (understanding) an event more clearly (one-third of respondents)

2) Resistance to life changes or **secondary gains** (such as losing disability money, avoid responsibility for doing more with one's life) (20%)

3) Limiting belief in one's ability to improve eyesight because of the 'natural aging process' or **disbelief that EFT could improve eyesight.** (nearly 18% of respondents)

Sample responses to the question *"what is the downside of improving your eyesight"* **were as follows:**

> *...if I can make this change - nothing is too impossible. Am I ready to accept that nothing is impossible?*

> *...Owning my power: if I could improve my eyesight with some simple tapping, then I would have to own my power - accept how powerful I really am.*

Q2. (The Biggest Reason...)

		Frequency	Percent	Valid Percent	Cumulative Percent
Valid	No reason/no reluctance	18	15.0	16.7	16.7
	Fear	36	30.0	**33.3**	50.0
	Resistance or secondary gain	22	18.3	**20.4**	70.4
	limiting belief	19	15.8	**17.6**	88.0
	Other reason	13	10.8	12.0	100.0
	Total	108	90.0	100.0	
Missing	No response	12	10.0		
Total		120	100.0		

Q3. Were you surprised about feelings and incidents from childhood that surfaced?

Those answering "yes" or "no" were equally distributed. One woman who answered yes stated, *"Yes, I was surprised that they had that kind of impact on my eyesight and health."*

Q3. (Surprised about feelings...)

		Frequency	Percent	Valid Percent	Cumulative Percent
Valid	No	49	40.8	**44.5**	44.5
	Yes	48	40.0	**43.6**	88.2
	Somewhat	7	5.8	6.4	94.5
	Nothing surfaced	6	5.0	5.5	100.0
	Total	110	91.7	100.0	
Missing	No response	10	8.3		
Total		120	100.0		

Many of those answering 'no' indicated that they actually had expected the tapping to unearth memories that would be related to their problems with their eyesight.

RESULTS FOR EACH INDICATOR OF CHANGE

Below you will find a chart for each indicator of change.

TOTAL represents the number of people who indicated a need for improvement in each particular area.

VALID PERCENT indicates the percentage of people who made an improvement anywhere between 15—100%. The participants were able to indicate levels of improvement through the following rating system:

0 = No change or improvement
1 = Very little improvement (up to 15%)
2 = Slight improvement (between 15-25%)
3 = Noticeable improvement (between 25-50%)
4 = Definite improvement (between 50-75%)
5 = Significant improvement (75% or more)

ABILITY TO SEE BRIGHTNESS:

In the following table, 60 people indicated that they had a problem seeing "brightness." At the end of the experiment, after taking out the answers indicating "very little change" (up to 15%), **over 41% identified a change between a slight and significant improvement (anywhere from 15% to over 75%).**

Brightness

		Frequency	Percent	Valid Percent	Cumulative Percent
Valid	No change	23	19.2	38.3	38.3
	Very little	12	10.0	20.0	58.3
	Slight	6	5.0	**10.0**	68.3
	Noticeable	10	8.3	**16.7**	85.0
	Definite	6	5.0	**10.0**	95.0
	Significant	3	2.5	**5.0**	100.0
	Total	**60**	50.0	100.0	
Missing	Non-applicable	60	50.0		
Total		120	100.0		

CLARITY OF NEAR VISION:

In the category for clarity, I asked participants to identify issues with clarity in their distance vision as well as in near vision, such as when they were reading. Sixty-eight (68) participants, or 56 per cent of the final group, indicated that they had trouble with their vision when reading or viewing up close. Of this group, **41% of them reported between 15-75% improvement in their near vision.** (Again, I did not include those that indicated less than a 15% improvement.)

Clarity (near)

		Frequency	Percent	Valid Percent	Cumulative Percent
Valid	No change	27	22.5	39.7	39.7
	Very little	13	10.8	19.1	58.8
	Slight	11	9.2	**16.2**	75.0
	Noticeable	9	7.5	**13.2**	88.2
	Definite	5	4.2	**7.4**	95.6
	Significant	3	2.5	**4.4**	100.0
	Total	**68**	56.7	100.0	
Missing	Non-applicable	52	43.3		
Total		120	100.0		

CLARITY OF FAR VISION:

In the chart below reporting on distance vision, **43% of the participants reported an improvement between 15-75%. And of this group,** *7.5% of them reported more than 75% improvement in their far sighted vision.*

Clarity (far)

		Frequency	Percent	Valid Percent	Cumulative Percent
Valid	No change	29	24.2	43.3	43.3
	Very little	9	7.5	13.4	56.7
	Slight	13	10.8	**19.4**	76.1
	Noticeable	6	5.0	**9.0**	85.1
	Definite	5	4.2	**7.5**	92.5
	Significant	5	4.2	**7.5**	100.0
	Total	**67**	55.8	100.0	
Missing	Non-applicable	53	44.2		
Total		120	100.0		

EYE FATIGUE:

In the next chart, you will notice that 33 people initially reported they had problems with eye fatigue. After the experiment, **nearly three-quarters of them reported that their eye fatigue had improved between 15 –75%.**

FATIGUE

		Frequency	Percent	Valid Percent	Cumulative Percent
Valid	Very little	9	7.5	27.3	27.3
	Slight	6	5.0	**18.2**	45.5
	Noticeable	10	8.3	**30.3**	75.8
	Definite	6	5.0	**18.2**	93.9
	Significant	2	1.7	**6.1**	100.0
	Total	**33**	27.5	100.0	
Missing	Non-applicable	87	72.5		
Total		120	100.0		

COLOR PERCEPTION:

In the results for "color perception" below, 50 people identified this as a problem, **and 38% of them reported an improvement somewhere between 15-75%.**

Color Perception

		Frequency	Percent	Valid Percent	Cumulative Percent
Valid	No change	21	17.5	42.0	42.0
	Very little	10	8.3	20.0	62.0
	Slight	6	5.0	**12.0**	74.0
	Noticeable	5	4.2	**10.0**	84.0
	Definite	5	4.2	**10.0**	94.0
	Significant	3	2.5	**6.0**	100.0
	Total	**50**	41.7	100.0	
Missing	Non-applicable	70	58.3		
Total		120	100.0		

COLOR CONTRAST:

Forty-nine participants indicated that noticing color contrast was an issue for them; **just under one-third of these people noticed a change from between 15%--over 75%.**

Color Contrast

		Frequency	Percent	Valid Percent	Cumulative Percent
Valid	No change	24	20.0	49.0	49.0
	Very little	10	8.3	20.4	69.4
	Slight	4	3.3	**8.2**	77.6
	Noticeable	3	2.5	**6.1**	83.7
	Definite	7	5.8	**14.3**	98.0
	Significant	1	.8	**2.0**	100.0
	Total	**49**	40.8	100.0	
Missing	Non-applicable	71	59.2		
Total		120	100.0		

DRYNESS

Forty-seven respondents indicated that dry eyes were a problem for them. Of these, nearly 47% indicated improvement of 15-over 75% by the end of the study.

DRYNESS

		Frequency	Percent	Valid Percent	Cumulative Percent
Valid	No change	19	15.8	40.4	40.4
	Very little	6	5.0	12.8	53.2
	Slight	12	10.0	**25.5**	78.7
	Noticeable	7	5.8	**14.9**	93.6
	Definite	3	2.5	**6.4**	100.0
	Total	**47**	39.2	100.0	
Missing	Non-applicable	73	60.8		
Total		120	100.0		

EYE BURNING/ ITCHING:

Of the 37 people who said that they were bothered by eye burning or itching, nearly one-third of those showed an improvement of between 15-75%.

EYE BURNING/ ITCHING

		Frequency	Percent	Valid Percent	Cumulative Percent
Valid	No change	18	15.0	48.6	48.6
	Very little	7	5.8	18.9	67.6
	Slight	3	2.5	**8.1**	75.7
	Noticeable	5	4.2	**13.5**	89.2
	Definite	4	3.3	**10.8**	100.0
	Total	**37**	30.8	100.0	
Missing	Non-applicable	83	69.2		
Total		120	100.0		

EYE STRAIN:

Of the 47 people who said they were bothered by eye strain, **nearly half of them indicated that they found improvement by the end of the experiment in the range of 15-over 75%.**

EYE STRAIN

		Frequency	Percent	Valid Percent	Cumulative Percent
Valid	No change	18	15.0	38.3	38.3
	Very little	7	5.8	14.9	53.2
	Slight	9	7.5	**19.1**	72.3
	Noticeable	9	7.5	**19.1**	91.5
	Definite	3	2.5	**6.4**	97.9
	Significant	1	.8	**2.1**	100.0
	Total	**47**	39.2	100.0	
Missing	Non-applicable	73	60.8		
Total		120	100.0		

FLOATERS:

While 34 people reported that they experienced "floaters" in their eyes, **29% of those that tracked this problem reported between a slight (15-25%) and significant (75% and above) improvement.**

FLOATERS (DECREASED)

		Frequency	Percent	Valid Percent	Cumulative Percent
Valid	No change	22	18.3	64.7	64.7
	Very little	2	1.7	5.9	70.6
	Slight	4	3.3	**11.8**	82.4
	Noticeable	3	2.5	**8.8**	91.2
	Definite	3	2.5	**8.8**	100.0
	Total	**34**	28.3	100.0	
Missing	Non-applicable	86	71.7		
Total		120	100.0		

- **Over 28% of the participants sought additional support from an EFT practitioner during the course of the experiment.**

- **For 30% of participants, the most significant change *reported* was in their vision.**

- **For another 46%, the most significant change *reported* was in the area of emotional release.**

Changes in the problems of <u>Nearsightedness</u> and <u>Farsightedness</u> are listed below.

Nearsightedness Change

		Frequency	Percent	Valid Percent	Cumulative Percent
Valid	No change	52	43.3	44.4	44.4
	Better	59	49.2	**50.4**	94.9
	Worse	6	5.0	5.1	100.0
	Total	**117**	97.5	100.0	
Missing	Not reported	3	2.5		
Total		120	100.0		

Over one-half of the participants indicated that their nearsightedness improved.

Farsightedness Change

		Frequency	Percent	Valid Percent	Cumulative Percent
Valid	No change	57	47.5	52.8	52.8
	Better	46	38.3	**42.6**	95.4
	Worse	5	4.2	4.6	100.0
	Total	**108**	90.0	100.0	
Missing	Not reported	12	10.0		
Total		120	100.0		

Over 42% of the participants who reported being farsighted, indicated an improvement.

LIMITATIONS of the EXPERIMENT / EXPERIMENTER:

While I am extremely satisfied with the results of the **EFT Eyesight Experiment**, I want to list some obvious limitations of this experiment and of me, Carol Look, the one conducting the experiment. As Gary would say, this experiment is a "good start."

(1) **There was no way to monitor participants' tapping.** Some may have been doing it in a quiet, peaceful place (as recommended with each week's assignments) while others may have had family, television or other distractions during their tapping sessions.

(2) **If a participant was "STUCK" or needing to go further on a particular issue,** I was unable to help the participants individually.

(3) **If any of the participants bumped into huge limiting beliefs not included in what I asked them to tap for,** there would be no chance of "collapsing" these beliefs if they were outside of conscious awareness. As we know now, limiting beliefs cause psychological reversal, and play a huge part in determining whether someone succeeds or not in making gains with **EFT.**

(4) **Some participants had problems with what I asked *or failed to ask* them to do.** Some responses were as follows:

   a. **I (Carol) did not account for the mid range of vision,** i.e. viewing a computer screen. (Many participants included computer viewing in "near" vision.)

   b. Someone complained that **I did not give them "permission" to tap more than once a day.** I was looking for compliance,

141

knowing if I asked for more than once a day, the compliance rate might have decreased.

c.   There was no allowance for eyesight problems GETTING WORSE, which we know can happen with symptoms when we tap on serious emotional conflict. As Gary tells us, when symptoms get worse, this is a good indicator that we are in the right "zone" and more emotional tapping should be done.

SUGGESTIONS FOR FURTHER STUDY:

The present experiment constitutes a preliminary pilot investigation. It would be very desirable to follow it up with some formal studies investigating, among other things, the following unanswered questions:

1. **To be a controlled experiment the study would need to include a comparison group** consisting of people with similar vision problems who do *not* receive any **EFT** treatment for 8 weeks. The responses of these people would be studied before and after this 8 week period in order to find out if any improvement occurred spontaneously over time (or if any symptom worsened).

2. It would also be valuable to obtain some **objective evidence** of the changes reported in the experiment by having formal eye examinations administered before the participants learn **EFT** and again 8 weeks after learning it, with the results formally compared by a vision specialist.

3. In addition, **"expectation effects" could be at least partially ruled out** by providing a third group of participants who did not know **EFT** and had absolutely no positive expectations concerning it. This would help to rule out the effects of positive suggestion.

4. **The high dropout rate in this experiment should also be investigated.** This might be done by comparing the dropout rate in the present experiment with the dropout rate of a group people practicing **EFT** for reasons quite unrelated to vision (who also used written instructions). It would also be desirable to include questionnaires concerning the reasons for the dropout rate in more detail in order to study the correlations between the tendency to drop out of the study and such factors as negative

reactions to the **EFT** process itself or to emotional material being unearthed that the participant found difficult to deal with, etc.

(All of these factors could be formally studied, producing a publishable study, if sufficient funding were available.)

MUST-SEE WEB SITES

For ongoing training and workshops in **EFT**, please visit the following web sites:

www.emofree.com – Hosted by **EFT** founder, Gary Craig, this exceptionally generous web site offers articles, case studies, research reports, practitioner referrals, approved workshops, original writings, theories and more. In addition, Gary offers an excellent tutorial program, the original free downloadable **EFT** manual and superb training DVDs and CDs.

www.CarolLook.com – Hosted by this book's author, this web site offers you dozens of **EFT** case studies, *Attracting Abundance with EFT* products (e-book, paperback book, special discount package, CDs and teleclasses), weight loss products, the field's classic quit smoking manual, a free *Attracting Abundance* newsletter and more. You may also access archives of Carol's internet radio show, *"Attracting Abundance: The Energy of Success"* where she interviews leaders in the field of Energy Psychology.

www.EFTupdate.com – Hosted by **EFT Master** and **EFT CHOICES** founder, Dr. Patricia Carrington, this web site provides certificate training programs (**EFT-CC** and **EFT-ADV**) for **EFT**, a referral network, the new computerized **EFT** program, *The Key to Successful Weight Loss* (with co-author Carol Look), and more.

www.ThrivingNow.com – Emotional freedom coach and certified massage therapist Rick Wilkes focuses on helping individuals in physical, emotional and spiritual pain to transform those energies into optimal health using a variety of techniques, especially **EFT**. He also offers an excellent membership program, and hosts weekly teleclasses.

www.EFT-Talk.com – Hosted by Carol Look and Rick Wilkes, this recently launched web site delivers weekly **EFT** podcasts to help you raise your vibration by combining **EFT** with the intentional use of the ***Law of Attraction***.

www.EFT4PowerPoint.com – Hosted by the director of the **EFT** Master program, Ann Adams, this web site sells the premier **EFT** for Power Point program for schools, organizations, and clinics.

ABOUT THE AUTHOR

Carol Look's specialty is inspiring clients to **attract abundance** into their lives by using **EFT** to clear limiting beliefs, release resistance, and build their "prosperity consciousness." Before becoming trained in numerous **Energy Psychology** methods, Carol was trained as a **Clinical Social Worker** and earned her Doctoral Degree in **Clinical Hypnotherapy**. She was one of the first practitioners in the world to be certified by **EFT** founder Gary Craig as an **EFT Master**.

Dr. Look worked as an addictions specialist for eight years at Freedom Institute, an out-patient substance abuse facility in New York City. She currently maintains a private practice and leads **EFT** workshops around the country on the topics of *Attracting Abundance, Anxiety Relief, Clearing Addictions*, and *Weight Loss*. She has been invited to teach **EFT** classes for organizations such as the *National Guild of Hypnotists* (**NGH**), the *Association of Comprehensive Energy Psychology* (**ACEP**), the *National Institute for the Clinical Application of Behavioral Medicine* (**NICABM**), the *Toronto Energy Psychology Conference* (**Toronto-EPC**) and the *Center for Spirituality and Psychotherapy* (**CSP**).

While Carol is no longer accepting new clients due to her extensive waiting list, she offers a wide variety of *Attracting Abundance with EFT* teleclasses, "live" workshops, and a variety of *abundance packages* for clients who are ready to break through any barriers to prosperity and expand their comfort zones.

Carol's new book, **Attracting Abundance with EFT**, is also available as an e-Book with companion audio recordings. Carol is the author of two of the field's classic **EFT** training manuals, **How To Lose Weight with Energy Therapy** and **Quit Smoking Now with Energy Therapy**. She is the senior author of the new computerized **EFT** program, **The Key to Successful Weight Loss**.

Carol hosts the popular internet radio show *Attracting Abundance: The Energy of Success*. Archives of the weekly show, including interviews with **EFT** Founder Gary Craig, Life Coach and *New York Times* bestselling author Cheryl Richardson, Internet Marketing genius Joe Vitale and others may be accessed by visiting www.CarolLook. com.

LaVergne, TN USA
17 September 2010
197317LV00002B/2/A

9 781425 949587